Communications
in Computer and Information Science   802

Commenced Publication in 2007
Founding and Former Series Editors:
Alfredo Cuzzocrea, Xiaoyong Du, Orhun Kara, Ting Liu, Dominik Ślęzak,
and Xiaokang Yang

Editorial Board

Simone Diniz Junqueira Barbosa
  Pontifical Catholic University of Rio de Janeiro (PUC-Rio),
  Rio de Janeiro, Brazil
Phoebe Chen
  La Trobe University, Melbourne, Australia
Joaquim Filipe
  Polytechnic Institute of Setúbal, Setúbal, Portugal
Igor Kotenko
  St. Petersburg Institute for Informatics and Automation of the Russian
  Academy of Sciences, St. Petersburg, Russia
Krishna M. Sivalingam
  Indian Institute of Technology Madras, Chennai, India
Takashi Washio
  Osaka University, Osaka, Japan
Junsong Yuan
  Nanyang Technological University, Singapore, Singapore
Lizhu Zhou
  Tsinghua University, Beijing, China

W0230404

More information about this series at http://www.springer.com/series/7899

Viviane Almeida dos Santos
Gustavo Henrique Lima Pinto
Adolfo Gustavo Serra Seca Neto (Eds.)

Agile Methods

8th Brazilian Workshop, WBMA 2017
Belém, Brazil, September 13–14, 2017
Revised Selected Papers

 Springer

Editors
Viviane Almeida dos Santos
Federal University of Pará
Tucurui
Brazil

Adolfo Gustavo Serra Seca Neto
Federal University of Technology
Paraná
Brazil

Gustavo Henrique Lima Pinto
Federal University of Pará
Belém
Brazil

ISSN 1865-0929   ISSN 1865-0937   (electronic)
Communications in Computer and Information Science
ISBN 978-3-319-73672-3   ISBN 978-3-319-73673-0   (eBook)
https://doi.org/10.1007/978-3-319-73673-0

Library of Congress Control Number: 2017963762

© Springer International Publishing AG 2018
This work is subject to copyright. All rights are reserved by the Publisher, whether the whole or part of the material is concerned, specifically the rights of translation, reprinting, reuse of illustrations, recitation, broadcasting, reproduction on microfilms or in any other physical way, and transmission or information storage and retrieval, electronic adaptation, computer software, or by similar or dissimilar methodology now known or hereafter developed.
The use of general descriptive names, registered names, trademarks, service marks, etc. in this publication does not imply, even in the absence of a specific statement, that such names are exempt from the relevant protective laws and regulations and therefore free for general use.
The publisher, the authors and the editors are safe to assume that the advice and information in this book are believed to be true and accurate at the date of publication. Neither the publisher nor the authors or the editors give a warranty, express or implied, with respect to the material contained herein or for any errors or omissions that may have been made. The publisher remains neutral with regard to jurisdictional claims in published maps and institutional affiliations.

Printed on acid-free paper

This Springer imprint is published by Springer Nature
The registered company is Springer International Publishing AG
The registered company address is: Gewerbestrasse 11, 6330 Cham, Switzerland

Preface

The 8th Brazilian Workshop on Agile Methods (WBMA 2017) was part of the Agile Brazil Conference. In 2017, the workshop was held in Belém, Pará, Brazil, during September 13–14. The workshop is the academic research track of the Agile Brazil Conference. The 2017 edition received 19 paper submissions and an impressive number of attendees (students, researchers, and practitioners) from different countries. This year, the workshop also strongly encouraged practitioners' submissions as a way to integrate and strengthen the conference target audience (industry and academy) relationships.

The submitted papers were peer reviewed by three referees. The paper-review process considered technical quality, relevance, significance, clarity, and concision. The Steering Committee decided to accept ten full papers and four short papers. However, two of the short papers were not presented at the workshop, and we had to exclude them from the WBMA 2017 proceedings. Thus, this CCIS volume comprises revised selected peer-reviewed versions of ten full papers and two short papers. The accepted papers present empirical studies on: agile values and principles; agile practices; agile adoption; agile testing and quality; metrics; conceptual studies; cultural aspects on agile business; organizational transformation and future trends.

The organizers thank the Program Committee members for their valuable contributions, the Agile Brazil organizers and sponsors, and especially all those who submitted papers to the workshop. We also thank Springer for producing the WBMA 2017 proceedings.

November 2017

Adolfo Gustavo Serra Seca Neto
Gustavo Henrique Lima Pinto
Viviane Almeida dos Santos

Organization

Steering Committee

Gustavo Henrique Lima Pinto	Federal University of Pará, Brazil
Viviane Almeida dos Santos	Federal University of Pará, Brazil
Adolfo Gustavo Serra Seca Neto	Federal University of Technology Paraná, Brazil

Program Committee

Ademar Aguiar	University of Porto, Portugal
Adolfo Gustavo Serra Seca Neto	Universidade Tecnológica Federal do Paraná, Brazil
Alexandre Vasconcelos	Universidade Federal de Pernambuco, Brazil
Alfredo Goldman	University of São Paulo, Brazil
Breno de França	Universidade de Campinas, Brazil
Célio Santana	Universidade Federal de Pernambuco, Brazil
Cleidson de Souza	Universidade Federal do Pará, Brazil
Eduardo Guerra	National Institute of Space Research, Brazil
Fabio Kon	Universidade de São Paulo, Brazil
Fábio Levy Siqueira	Escola Politécnica da Universidade de São Paulo, Brazil
Felipe Furtado	Universidade Federal de Pernambuco, C.E.S.A.R, Brazil
Graziela Tonin	Universidade Federal de Pernambuco, Brazil
Gustavo Pinto	Universidade Federal do Pará, Brazil
Hugo Sereno Ferreira	FEUP and INESC TEC, Brazil
Jutta Eckstein	IT Communication, Germany
Maria Istela Cagnin	Universidade Federal do Mato Grosso do Sul, Brazil
Patrícia Vilain	Universidade Federal de Santa Catarina, Brazil
Paulo Meirelles	Universidade de Brasília, Brazil
Rafael Prikladnicki	PUCRS, Brazil
Rodrigo De Toledo	UFRJ, Brazil
Sandro Oliveira	Universidade Federal do Pará, Brazil
Teresa Maciel	Universidade Federal Rural de Pernambuco, Brazil
Theodore D. Hellmann	USA
Tiago Silva Da Silva	Universidade Federal de São Paulo, Brazil
Vinicius Garcia	Universidade Federal de Pernambuco, Brazil
Viviane Almeida dos Santos	Universidade Federal do Pará, Brazil
Xiaofeng Wang	Free University of Bozen-Bolzano, Italy

Conference Logo

Sponsors

Contents

Conceptual Studies and Theoretical Foundations of Agile/Lean

Organizational Transformation and Cultural Aspects on Agile Business

Agile Practices and Future Trends, Evolution and Revolution (Technical or Managerial)

Agile Principles, Lean Manufacturing and Other Disciplines

Towards a Definition of Simplicity in Agile Software Development: A Focus Group Study

Wylliams B. Santos[1,2]([⊠]), José Adson O. G. Cunha[3]([⊠]), Hermano Moura[1]([⊠]), and Tiziana Margaria[4]([⊠])

[1] Centre for Informatics, Federal University of Pernambuco,
Recife, Pernambuco, Brazil
{wbs,hermano}@cin.ufpe.br
[2] University of Pernambuco, Caruaru, Pernambuco, Brazil
[3] Exact Sciences Department, Federal University of Paraíba,
João Pessoa, Paraíba, Brazil
adson@dcx.ufpb.br
[4] University of Limerick and Lero - The Irish Software Research Centre,
Limerick, Ireland
tiziana.margaria@lero.ie

Abstract. Although Agile Software Development (ASD) has proven to be an important set of methods that promotes simplicity issues, there are difficulties in defining simplicity. In order to develop a conceptual model of simplicity from the agile teams perspective, a literature review was conducted covering models related to simplicity in different research areas. Based on that, a conceptual model was developed, which was then triangulated through a focus group with six ASD experts. Five simplicity perspectives in the context of ASD were identified. From the agile teams perspective, simplicity is defined as the theoretical virtue disposing the team towards an analytic attitude that leads agile projects to be successful. The conceptual model of simplicity in agile software development is an invitation to practitioners to do what they already do, but to do so more consciously. This consciousness can make a substantial difference in real situations.

Keywords: Simplicity · Agile software development · Focus group

1 Introduction

Considering the emerging challenges and opportunities in software development, Agile Software Development (ASD) represents an alternative to the heavyweight methodologies. It puts less emphasis on up-front and strict control and relies more on informal collaboration, coordination, and learning [1,2].

According to the Agile Manifesto [3], the ASD demands a focus on simplicity stating that it is essential. Although there is a variety of methodologies and frameworks of ASD (eXtreme Programming, Scrum, Lean Software Development, Feature-Driven Development, and Crystal methodologies), few academic

© Springer International Publishing AG 2018
V. A. Santos et al. (Eds.): WBMA 2017, CCIS 802, pp. 3–17, 2018.
https://doi.org/10.1007/978-3-319-73673-0_1

studies directly address simplicity [4–8]. In order to provide a better under-standing of simplicity, this work proposes a definition of simplicity from the agile team's perspective and a conceptual model based on a literature review which were then triangulated with experts through a focus group.

The remainder of this paper is organised as follows. Section 2 introduces the background and related work of simplicity in three domains: Philosophy, Infor-mation and Communications Technology (ICT), and Agile Software Develop-ment. Section 3 presents the research method and the focus group conducted with practitioners and researchers. Section 4 presents the conceptual model underly-ing simplicity definition from the agile team's perspective. Section 5 discusses the limitations and implications for practices of our study. Finally, Sect. 6 addresses conclusions and opportunities for future works.

2   Theoretical Background

The study of simplicity is an interdisciplinary endeavor with many concepts and attributes. Margaria et al. [9] emphasises that the concept of simplicity is by far not a simple concept because there are many perspectives on the perception of simplicity.

2.1   Simplicity in Philosophy

Simplicity principles have been proposed in various forms by theologians, philoso-phers, and scientists, from ancient to modern times. There is a widespread philo-sophical presumption that simplicity is a theoretical virtue. This presumption that simpler theories are preferable appears in many guises [10,11]. According to Gambrel and Cafaro [10], virtue refers to the generic term commonly used for any character trait people wish to commend. In both common speech and philo-sophical discourse, the virtues refer to those qualities whose possession makes a person, a good person.

Additionally, following Nussbaums schema [12], Gambrel and Cafaro [10] define simplicity as the virtue disposing us to act appropriately within the sphere of our consumer decisions. From this point of view, simplicity is a conscien-tious and restrained attitude toward material goods that typically includes (i) decreased consumption and (ii) a more conscious consumption, (iii) greater delib-eration regarding our consumer decision, (iv) a more focused life in general, and (v) a greater and more nuance appreciation for other things besides material goods.

2.2   Simplicity in Information and Communications Technology

According to Margaria and Hinchey [5], the culture of "less" can be profoundly disruptive, cutting out existing "standard" elements from products and busi-ness models, thereby revolutionising entire markets. Ebert [13] affirms that what determines a product's success isn't the number of features; it's the few features

Table 1. Dimensions of simplicity [4,9].

Dimension	Description
The art of knowing	Knowing about an IT system, the more simple it appears to that user
Structure	The notions of layering and decomposition boundaries direct the focus to a smaller subset of the problem thus leading towards a simpler problem domain
Orthogonality	Systems where the components are orthogonal, and the results are predictable are viewed as simpler IT systems. This design concept is keenly important when dealing with modularisation
Size	The goal of simplicity in IT is to reduce aspects of systems, such as the number of functions offered, the number of modules, to the core ones desired by users
Transparency	Transparent systems which explicit their assumptions are perceived as being simpler
Predictability	Systems whose behaviour and structure are predictable are perceived to be simpler. The early feedback contributes to eliminate, or at least to mitigate through early discovery, the surprises in the systems
Communication	Transparency and predictability taken together led often to the fundamental question of how much, how, and when to communicate
Automation	Simplicity is also characterised as a measure of how little the end user has to do
Abstraction	By focusing on a right set of concepts and relationships, one can highlight the essence of the problem that needs to be addressed
Context and Subjectivity (felt complexity)	Simplicity does not so much relate to a problem as such, but rather to the way how this is perceived by the various stakeholders

that differentiate it from other products. Complexity scales must be mastered with product strategy, sound engineering process, and technology management to achieve the necessary simplicity that secures the growth and sustains the markets.

The predominant philosophy is that simplicity "is about subtracting the obvious, and adding the meaningful". Based on models of simplicity and findings resulted from a Systematic Literature Review and direct interaction with experts (individual interviews and focus group) in the area of ICT, Margaria, Floyd, Bernhard and Bosselmann [4,9] compiled evidences (a set of recommendations) for possible lines of action, characterisation and dimensions of simplicity, as presented in Table 1. These studies support that the philosophy of simplicity is strategically important, yet still insufficiently understood.

2.3   Simplicity in Agile Software Development

Based on the evolution of Project Management (PM) thinking, Moura and Skibniewski [14] presented the Software Project Framework (SPF), composed of disciplines, principles and dimensions in order to verify how PM and related research have evolved over the years and to identify related trends. Simplicity is one of the 14 dimensions (directions) for advancing research proposed by the SPF. Moura and Skibniewski considered the agile methods as a promising approach to this dimension.

In order to satisfy the agile values, some principles[1] should be respected, including that "Simplicity, the art of maximising the amount of work not done, is essential". Various methods propose agility in their definitions, aiming to find efficient ways for developing software of quality across an agile development process. In essence, agile methods emphasise simplicity. The goal is to get user feedback quickly by delivering software at short increments, even if it covers only a subset of the expected functionality [15].

Additionally, Meyer [15] affirms that who has ever obtained the first solution to a problem of any kind, found it complex, and tried to simplify it. Therefore, achieving simplicity often means adding work, sometimes lots of it. From this point of view, achieving simplicity is not the same as minimising work [16].

Lean [17] also puts a very strong emphasis on simplicity. Lean comes from Lean Manufacturing and is a set of principles for achieving quality, speed and costumer alignment. Poppendieck and Poppendieck [18] adapted the principles from Lean Manufacturing to fit software development. The Lean principle of eliminate waste is supported and discussed by some empirical studies [19,20]. Zanoni et al. [19] extend the definition of waste to fit in the software intensive product development context. More recently, in 2017, Sedano, Ralph and Péraire identified and described different types of waste in software development: building the wrong feature or product, mismanaging the backlog, rework, unnecessarily complex solutions, extraneous cognitive load, psychological distress, waiting/multitasking, knowledge loss, and ineffective communication.

In this space, this research work provides the definition of simplicity in agile software development and a conceptual model that support its definition. In this sense, it is an invitation to practitioners to do what they already do, but to do so more consciously. This consciousness can make a substantial difference in real situations. From this perspective, rethinking means committing oneself to a course of action where plausible analysis exists, to reexamine the adopted practices focused on simplicity.

3   Research Method

Our conceptual model of simplicity in ASD was based on the general process (Fig. 1). The first step, Literature Review, embodies the initial literature review

---

[1] http://agilemanifesto.org/principles.html.

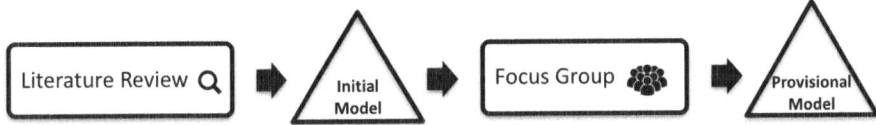

Fig. 1. Research design.

(Sect. 2), gathering knowledge of ASD and the key concepts in the field of simplicity, with emphasis on the agile software development aspects. Based on the early findings from the literature review, an initial conceptual model and simplicity definition from agile team's perspective is proposed (Sect. 4.1). The second step, Focus Group, addresses the focus group session performed to evaluate the main elements and relationships proposed in the Initial model step. The Provisional Model (Sect. 4.2) is dedicated to incorporate and improve the model based on the focus group and literature review.

As a method of qualitative research data collection, a focus group is an interview on a topic with a group of people who have knowledge of the topic [21,22]. Since the data we obtained from a focus group is socially constructed within obtaining feedback on specific the group, a interpretivist (constructivism) perspective underlies this data collection procedure.

In this sense, this research adopts the main steps of the guideline for conducting and discussing focus group sessions in software engineering research proposed by Kontio [23]. Following, we provide more information about the design and arrangements of the study.

3.1   Defining the Research Problem

This study aim is to obtain an in-depth feedback on the proposed definition of simplicity, generating ideas, collecting, prioritising potential problems, discovering underlying ground and motivations. Furthermore, our focus group session also centralises attention on obtaining feedback on specific elements of our conceptual model underlying simplicity from the agile team's perspective.

3.2   Selecting the Participants

According to Kontio [23], the value of the method is very sensitive to the experience and insight of the participants. Thus recruiting representative, insightful and motivated participants is critical to the success of a focus group study. In this sense, we purposely sampled six high qualified researchers and practitioners in ASD with different roles, such as project manager, consultant, professor, researcher, scrum master and Project Manager Officer (PMO) with different genders, ages and levels of education, to achieve maximum variation in data collection. We considered only PhD researchers in the project management area. Table 2 compiles the participants' demographic profile.

Table 2. Profile of participants

	Role	Education	Gender	PM (years)	Agile (years)	Agile methods	Certification
P1	Researcher Consultant Professor Scrum Master	PhD	Male	6 to 10	6 to 10	Scrum Kanban LSD	CSM
P2	Project Manager Researcher Professor Scrum Master	PhD	Male	16 to 20	11 to 15	Scrum Kanban LSD ASD MAnGve [24]	CSM ITIL COBIT
P3	Consultant Researcher Professor Scrum Master	PhD	Male	11 to 15	6 to 10	Scrum XP	CSM CSPO MPS.BR
P4	PMO Manager Researcher Professor Scrum Master	PhD	Male	11 to 15	6 to 10	Scrum Kanban	PMP
P5	Consultant Researcher Professor Scrum Master	PhD	Female	6 to 10	6 to 10	Scrum Kanban	CSM CSD MPS.BR CERTICS
P6	Researcher Professor Scrum Master	PhD	Male	6 to 10	6 to 10	Scrum XP	PMP CSM

Due to anonymity and ethical issues, the participants are labelled by *P1* to *P6* codes. All of participants are Certified Scrum Master (CSM), with exception to *P4*, who is a Project Management Professional (PMP). Besides CSM and PMP, all participants are specialists in project management, governance and software quality. According to Table 2, they hold extensive industry certifications, including Certified Scrum Product Owner (CSPO), Certified Scrum Developer (CSD), Information Technology Infrastructure Library (ITIL), Control Objectives for Information and Related Technologies (COBIT), Certificate on Technology and Innovation in Brazil (CERTICS), and Brazilian Process Improvement Model (MPS.Br).

3.3   Planning and Conducting the Focus Group Session

We held a pilot session with two researchers, who is not included in those described in Table 2, in order to practice the focus group process and evaluate the questions. As a result, a few minor changes in question phrasing were made.

All the subjects agreed to participate in this focus group session and gave their written informed consent. The focus group session lasted 120 min and was recorded with an MP3 player. The use of audio recording ensured an identical replication of the session, thus facilitating its analysis.

The session started with an overview of the objectives of the study and full explanation about the nature of participation. The audio data of the session was transcribed by the investigator using oTranscribe[2] and analysed through ATLAS.ti[3]. Based on Kontio's guideline [23], the discussion transcript was issue-based, i.e., each issue or point raised was documented verbatim, but the transcript did not include clarification discussions, jokes, or other non-related communications in the meeting. Aiming to keep the anonymity and confidentiality, just the named investigators had access to the verbatim data collected during the session.

The first author of this paper worked as a facilitator of the session by motivating the participants to discuss and by leading the discussion. The interview script was composed of open-end questions. This kind of question is designed to encourage a full, meaningful answer using the subject's own knowledge. In order to reach the research problem (Sect. 3.1), we set out to answer the following research questions (RQs):

- *RQ1:* Is the definition of simplicity from the agile teams perspective understandable? Please explain.
- *RQ2:* Are the conceptual model and their elements which support the definition of simplicity from the agile teams perspective understandable?
- *RQ3:* Are the conceptual model and their elements which support the definition of simplicity from the agile teams perspective reasonable?

4   Conceptual Model

According to our literature review, we identified five simplicity perspectives in the context of Agile Software Development (see Fig. 2): agile team, product, project process, customer, and user. Each of these perspectives are following summarised.

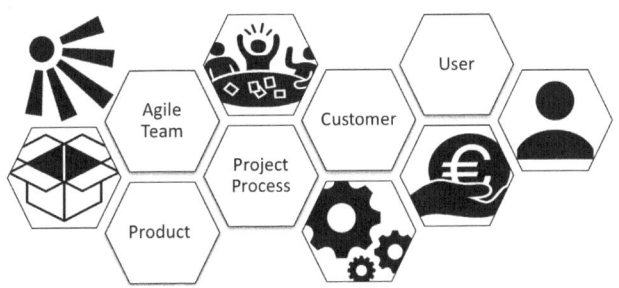

Fig. 2. Simplicity perspectives in agile software development.

---

[2] http://otranscribe.com.
[3] http://atlasti.com.

- Agile Team perspective addresses various aspects of team dynamics. e.g., organization and communication;
- Product perspective focuses on aspects regarding the software (value) that are developed. e.g., usability and easy integration;
- Project Process perspective is related to agile practises and techniques for managing and developing the project. e.g., delivery strategy and pair programming;
- Customer's viewpoint addresses aspects regarding the business requirements. e.g., coordination of financial side, product backlog and sprint planning meeting.
- Simplicity from the user's viewpoint addresses aspects regarding the user-experience (UX). e.g., you must first know the user and continually test your assumptions.

Additionally, our representation (see Fig. 2) is composed by a pictogram, which represents different viewpoints or perspectives of each dimension of simplicity. The proposed model is particularly interested in addressing agile team's point of view. Conforming to Margaria et al. [9] there are many perspectives on the concept of simplicity. For example, simplicity can be related to the number of components a system possesses. It can also reflect the amount of effort a user of the system has to expend to use the system or the level of effort and amount of knowledge to understand the system.

4.1   Initial Definition and Conceptual Model Based on a Literature Review

Outlining the diverse definitions from different areas, we defined simplicity from the agile team's perspective by adopting the ultimate function, rather than defining a set of practises. In this sense, we define simplicity in ASD as:

> "The theoretical virtue disposing the team towards a conscientious, minimalistic and analytic attitude that leads agile projects to be successful".

This definition was inspired by the functional definition of *agile* proposed by Kruchten [25]. He also illustrates a great analogy by defining a road: "*Would you define a road as something made of crushed rocks and tar, or define it as a surface that is black rather than white, flat rather than undulated, and with painted lines rather than monochrome? Or would you rather define a road as a component of a transportation system, allowing people and goods to be moved on the ground surface from point A to point B? And then let the properties or components of the road be derived from this functional definition, allowing some novel approaches in road design, rather than defining it narrowly using a common recipe.*" The same analogy is applied to our definition of simplicity from the perspective of the agile team.

Our conceptual model (See Fig. 3) is a coherent system of interrelated fundamentals that lead to consistent explanation regarding the definition of simplicity from the agile team's perspective. It is set up and inspired by Egyptian pyramids, certainly one of the most perfect and extraordinary shapes created by humans [26]. Additionally, the regular tetrahedron, comprising only four equilateral triangles, has a claim to simplicity and symmetry [27]. Analogously, these are the main characteristics of our pyramid.

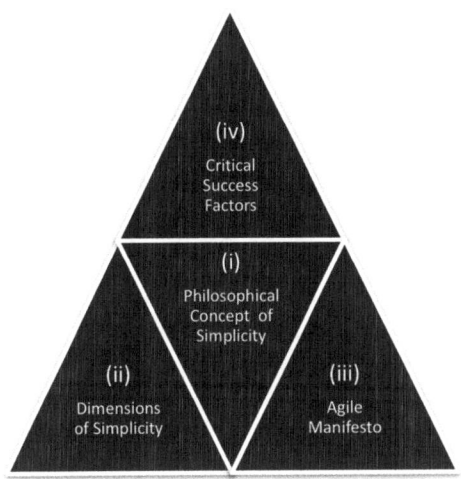

Fig. 3. Pyramid of simplicity in ASD.

Figure 3 provides an overview of the conceptual model illustrating the nature and relationships between the different components of the pyramid. The pyramid is revolving around the Agile Manifesto (iii), which unifies and establishes a common set of values and principles; (ii) dimensions of simplicity (Table 1), which identify the structures and aspects that lead to simplicity. On the top of the pyramid, (iv) Critical Success Factors [28] - are the factors that must be present for the agile project to be successful. The (i) philosophical concept of simplicity [10] is considered as the centre or as a core part of the model.

4.2 Provisional Conceptual Model and Definition Based on a Focus Group

A focus group session was conducted to triangulate the conceptual model and definition with experts. Participants were asked about their understanding of the proposed definition of simplicity in agile software development. The findings of this step are presented here. For each quote, the following format was adopted: *[P participant number]*. The main investigator acted as the moderator of the session with special care to not interfere in the discussion, just clarifying unclear issues.

The thematic analysis method was used for identifying, analysing, and reporting patterns (themes) within the transcribed data. Cruzes and Dybå [29] describe the main steps and checklist items proposed for thematic synthesis in Software Engineering: extract data, code data, translate codes into themes, create a model of higher-order themes, and access the trustworthiness of the synthesis. The thematic map relating the categories extracted during the focus group analysis are illustrated in Fig. 4 and described further below.

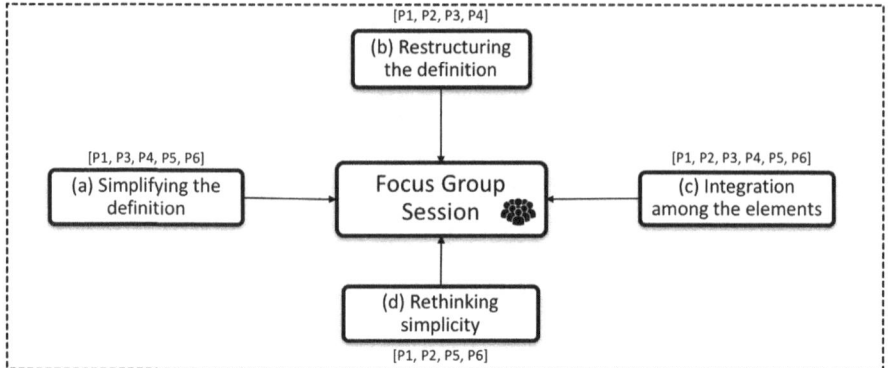

Fig. 4. Thematic map: Focus group session.

(a) Simplifying the Definition: All participants were clear in standing that simplicity in the context of ASD needs a simple definition. According to them, the proposed definition is not clear and some enhancement are necessary in order to keep the desired statement (simple as possible). As some participants strongly indicated:

> "the definition of simplicity in agile software development *must be simple.*" [P4]
> "There isn't a definition that the user can read and immediately understands, so we have to present additional explanations. The current setting is *complex.*"[P3]

Additionally, all experts state that according to the agile culture, simple definitions are preferred by the agile practitioners.

(b) Restructuring the Definition: All experts were headed towards a systemic restructuring of the definition, as indicated in the following quote.

> "... *restructure the definition* to make it cleaner (the way of writing). Make the *definition* less philosophical."[P5]

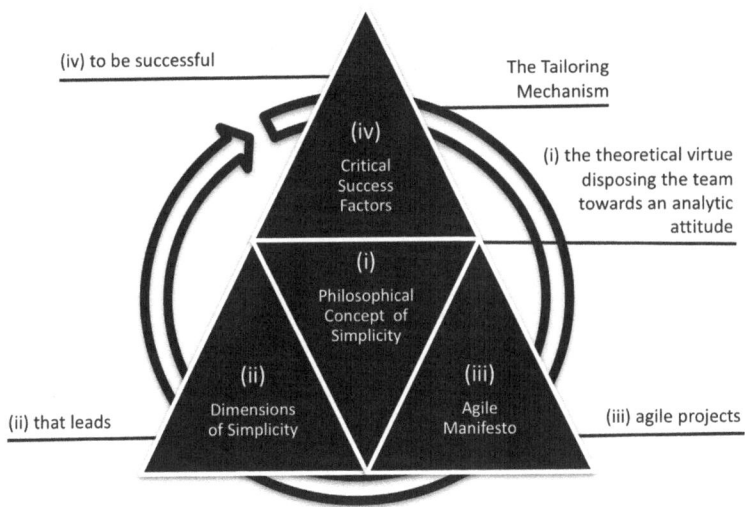

Fig. 5. Pyramid of simplicity in ASD: Relationship between the conceptual model and the tailoring mechanism.

(c) Integration Among the Elements: All experts claimed that all unit elements have to be in synergy towards simplicity, as indicated in the following excerpt:

> " the components (conceptual model) are coherent, but there must be a conceptual integration among them."[P2]

As can be seen in Fig. 5, the arrow involving the pyramid symbolises "the tailoring mechanism" of our conceptual model, which proposes an integration and accommodation of concepts among the different elements of our conceptual model: (i) philosophical concept of simplicity, (ii) dimensions of simplicity, (iii) agile manifesto, and (iv) critical success factors.

We argue that by incorporating the tailoring mechanism, an overarching concept-centric view of simplicity would allow practitioners and researchers to critically reflect on agile methods, and constantly find ways of extending or tailoring the method to foster and promote simplicity in order to continuous improvement.

(d) Rethinking Simplicity: This new way of dealing with simplicity in the context of agile software development requires the capacity to rethink the underlying competences under a different image of project, demanding a new team's mindset in order to further boost the success of the projects with focus on simplicity, as stated by one of our participants.

"it's an interesting topic. Both, researchers and practitioners must discuss, enrich and <u>*extend the topic of simplicity*</u> *beyond its current conceptual foundations".* [P1]

Furthermore, relationships between the components of the pyramid are not stated in a linear/sequential way. Essentially, they must be present in order to keep the "spirit of simplicity".

Provisional Definition and Model: Based on participants understanding and analysis resulted from the focus group session, some enhancements were needed in our proposed definition. As following, we present the amended definition. The new text is underlined and important deletions are indicated using strikethrough.

"the theoretical virtue disposing the team towards ~~*a conscientious, minimalistic and*~~ <u>*an*</u> *analytic attitude that leads agile projects to be successful".*

All participants were unanimous in emphasising that *conscientious* and *minimalistic* are embodied by the term *analytic attitude*. According to participants, a person who advocates or practises minimalism, automatically embodies an analytic attitude. Additionally, in order to proceed analytic attitude, a very seriously and conscientious postures are necessary. In this regards, these terms were removed from the provisional definition, stated as:

"the theoretical virtue disposing the team towards an analytic attitude that leads agile projects to be successful".

Each element of our definition is exploited in Fig. 5 as: (i) "the theoretical virtue disposing the team towards an analytic attitude" is related with the philosophical concept of simplicity (core of the pyramid); (ii) the term "that leads" addresses the connection with "Dimensions of Simplicity", the first base of the pyramid; (iii) "agile projects" refers to the values and principles of "Agile Manifesto", the second base of the pyramid; and (iv) "to be successful" is based on the Critical Success Factors triangle (top of the pyramid).

5   Discussion

In this section, we discuss the limitations, validity, and reliability of our results. Implications of the results for practice are also addressed.

5.1   Addressing Limitations, Validity and Reliability

The validity and reliability of our results are discussed from the perspective proposed by Merriam [30].

Construct validity in qualitative research is related to the precise and clearcut definition of constructs that is consistent with the meanings assigned by the research participants. Although we constantly compared and contrasted our construct definitions with the literature, another focus group session can be executed for obtaining additional qualitative insights and feedback from practitioners.

Internal validity, or *credibility*, is related to the extent that the results match reality. To increase credibility, we sampled experts in ASD with different roles in software projects, as described in Table 2. The preliminary results were discussed between the authors to refine the findings. In this sense, we reduced the potential bias in interpreting the results by having another person reviewing all interpretations made during the analysis. A limitation is that we conducted only one focus group session.

Reliability refers to the extent that the results can be replicated. We tried to provide a rich description of the research method, the context in which the research was performed, and the results themselves.

Finally, this study reflects the results from a focus group with six experts with different points of view and perceptions about the studied phenomenon. Although they contributed to a rich description of the definition, we aim to replicate our protocol in other cases.

5.2 Implications for Practice

The provisional conceptual model and definition of simplicity is proposed to be a careful tool to understand the simplicity phenomena in ASD. It aims to be useful and reflective in its approach to both researchers and practitioners.

In this regard, the practitioners that desire to achieve simplicity through a thoughtful way can be benefited to do what they already do, but to do so more consciously. As an example, from this analysis, some agile practices could be refocused and re-prioritised as a vehicle to promote effective results, disposing the agile team toward the focus on critical factors to project success.

This consciousness can make a substantial difference in real situations, because simplicity does relate to the way how this is perceived by the agile team. It can influence the actions that follow, and the eventual results that might be achieved. As usual, when building mindsets, awareness sharpens the sight, especially in critical situations.

6   Concluding Remarks and Future Works

Simplicity has been increasingly recognised as a driving paradigm in ICT development, maintenance, use and management, but according to the experts and the literature, there are difficulties in defining simplicity and its impact on projects.

This study is part of an ongoing research aimed to identify laws, practises, strategies, factors, techniques and theories in order to improve the simplicity management [7,8,31]. This article presents a conceptual model underlying simplicity definition from the agile team's perspective. We believe that an exhaustive comprehension of this phenomena could support academics and practitioners in the direction of increasing the success rates of projects.

Future works will focus on the development of a deeper knowledge and comprehensive understanding based on a Systematic Mapping Study. Qualitative studies will be conducted to understand how project managers and software engineers (developers) interpret their experiences about simplicity in ASD in the workplace. Besides, we aim to conduct another focus group session with developers as source of information to capture the agile team perspective.

Acknowledgements. The authors would like to acknowledge the Brazilian National Research Council - CNPq (142296/2013-9), Brazil's Science without Borders Program (205663/2014-1), the SFI grant 13/RC/2094 to Lero - the Irish Software Research Centre (www.lero.ie), and University of Limerick for the support of this research.

References

1. Dybå, T., Dingsøyr, T., Moe, N.B.: Agile project management. In: Ruhe, G., Wohlin, C. (eds.) Software Project Management in a Changing World, pp. 277–300. Springer, Heidelberg (2014). https://doi.org/10.1007/978-3-642-55035-5_11
2. Mello, R., Silva, P., Travassos, G.: Agilidade em Processos de Software: Evidências Sobre Características de Agilidade e Práticas Ágeis. In: XIII Brazilian Symposium on Software Quality (SBQS). Technical Papers, pp. 151–164. Brazilian Computer Society (SBC), Blumenau (2014)
3. Beck, K., Beedle, M.: Manifesto for agile software development (2001). http://agilemanifesto.org. Accessed 19 June 2017
4. Floyd, B.D., Bosselmann, S.: ITSy - simplicity research in information and communication technology. Computer **46**(11), 26–32 (2013)
5. Margaria, T., Hinchey, M.: Simplicity in IT: the power of less. Computer **46**(11), 23–25 (2013)
6. Margaria, T., Steffen, B.: Simplicity as a driver for agile innovation. Computer **43**(6), 90–92 (2010)
7. Santos, W., Perrelli, H.: Towards an approach to foster simplicity in agile software development projects. In: 9th Workshop on Information System PhD and Master's Thesis (12th Brazilian Symposium on Information Systems). SBSI 2016, Florianópolis-SC, Brazil, pp. 4–7. Association for Computing Machinery (ACM) (2016)
8. Santos, W.: Towards a better understanding of simplicity in agile software development projects. In: Proceedings of the 20th International Conference on Evaluation and Assessment in Software Engineering. EASE 2016, pp. 2:1–2:4. ACM, New York (2016)
9. Margaria, T., Floyd, B.D., Steffen, B.: ITSy - recommendation document. University of Postdam, Postdam, Technical report (2011). https://www.cs.uni-potsdam.de/gsse/ITSy/files/ITSy_final_report.pdf. Accessed 19 June 2017
10. Gambrel, J.C., Cafaro, P.: The virtue of simplicity. J. Agric. Environ. Ethics **23**, 85–108 (2009). VN-r
11. Baker, A.: Simplicity. The Standard Encyclopedia of Philosophy (2013). http://plato.stanford.edu/archives/fall2013/entries/simplicity/. Accessed 19 June 2017
12. Nussbaum, M.C.: Non-relative virtues: an aristotelian approach. Midwest Stud. Philos. **13**(1), 32–53 (1988)
13. Ebert, C., Hoefner, G., Mani, V.S.: What next? Advances in software-driven industries. IEEE **32**, 22–28 (2015)

14. Moura, H., Skibniewski, M.: The evolution of management thinking. In: International Research Network on Organizing by Project (IRNOP) (2011)
15. Meyer, B.: Agile! The Good, the Hype and the Ugly. Springer, Cham (2014). https://doi.org/10.1007/978-3-319-05155-0
16. Dingsøyr, T., Nerur, S., Balijepally, V., Moe, N.B.: A decade of agile methodologies: towards explaining agile software development. J. Syst. Softw. **85**(6), 1213–1221 (2012)
17. Womack, J.P., Jones, D.T.: Lean Thinking: Banish Waste and Create Wealth in Your Corporation, 2nd edn. Productivity Press, New York (2003)
18. Poppendieck, M., Poppendieck, T.: Lean Software Development: An Agile Toolkit. Addison-Wesley Longman Publishing Co., Inc., Boston (2003)
19. Zanoni, M., Perin, F., Fontana, F.A., Viscusi, G.: Extending value stream mapping through waste definition beyond customer perspective. J. Softw. Evol. Process **26**(12), 1172–1192 (2014)
20. Sedano, T., Ralph, P., Péraire, C.: Software development waste. In: 39th International Conference on Software Engineering - ICSE 2017, May 2017, pp. 130–140. IEEE Computer Society (2017)
21. Seaman, C.: Qualitative methods in empirical studies of software engineering. IEEE Trans. Software Eng. **25**(4), 557–572 (1999)
22. Runeson, P., Höst, M.: Guidelines for conducting and reporting case study research in software engineering. Empir. Softw. Eng. **14**(2), 131–164 (2009)
23. Kontio, J., Lehtola, L., Bragge, J.: Using the focus group method in software engineering: obtaining practitioner and user experiences. In: International Symposium on Empirical Software Engineering (ISESE 2004), pp. 271–280. IEEE Computer Society, Washington, DC (2004)
24. de Oliveria Luna, A.J.H., de Farias Junior, I.H., Kruchten, P., Moura, H.: MAnGve : a step towards deploying agile governance. In: Brazilian Symposium on Software Engineering (SBES) - Industry Track (CBSoft 2014), November, Maceió, AL, Brazil (2014)
25. Kruchten, P.: Contextualizing agile software development. J. Softw. Evol. Process **24**, 351–361 (2013)
26. Morris, G., Schadla-Hall, R.T.: Ancient Egypt on the small screen - from fact to fiction in the UK. In: Consuming Ancient Egypt, Chap. 14, pp. 195–215. UCL Press - Institute of Archaeology, London (2003). http://discovery.ucl.ac.uk/11409/. Accessed 19 June 2017
27. Humbert, J.-M., Price, C.: Imhotep Today: Engyptianizing Architecture. UCL Press - Institute of Archaeology, London (2003)
28. da Silva, K.M.B., dos Santos, S.C.: Critical factors in agile software projects according to people, process and technology perspective. In: 6th Brazilian Workshop on Agile Methods (WBMA 2015), Agile Brazil 2015, Porto de Galinhas (2015)
29. Cruzes, D.S., Dybå, T.: Recommended steps for thematic synthesis in software engineering. In: International Symposium on Empirical Software Engineering and Measurement, no. 7491, pp. 275–284 (2011)
30. Merriam, S.B.: Qualitative Research: A Guide to Design and Implementation. Jossey-Bass Higher and Adult Education Series, 2nd edn. Wiley, Hoboken (2009)
31. Moreira, B., Barbosa Santos, W., Júnior, I., Moura, H., Margaria, T.: Simplicidade no Desenvolvimento Ágil de Software: Resultados Preliminares de um Mapeamento Sistemático da Literatura. In: XIII Brazilian Symposium on Information Systems (SBSI), 4th Workshop on Information Systems Undergraduate Research (WICSI), pp. 89–92. Brazilian Computer Society (SBC), Lavras (2017)

Agile Testing and Quality: Techniques, Patterns and Automated Support

ASA: Agile Software Development Self-assessment Method

Matheus Florêncio, Fernando Sambinelli[✉], and Marcos Augusto Francisco Borges

Faculdade de Tecnologia, Universidade Estadual de Campinas,
Campus Limeira, R. Paschoal Marmo, 1888, Limeira, SP 13484-332, Brazil
m137014@dac.unicamp.br, f180172@g.unicamp.br,
marcosborges@ft.unicamp.br

Abstract. The migration from classical development to agile methodologies presents itself as a journey with many obstacles. New methods and tools for evaluating teams and organizations that support this process have been developed by the academic community and industry. However, questions have been raised on the inconsistencies for alignment of these methods with respect to the principles contained in the Agile Manifesto. The objective of this work was to investigate these possible inconsistencies and propose solutions in order to solve them. A critical analysis of the main agile evaluation methods and tools was carried out, based on a review of the literature, and misalignments were identified regarding the agile principles of flexibility, simplicity and pursuit for excellence. A new method of evaluation, the Agile Self-Assessment, has been proposed to address these gaps and to add to the capacity for continuous improvement in this process. A prototype tool was also developed that implements the method proposed in this work.

Keywords: Agile methodologies · Agile Manifesto · Continuous improvement

1 Introduction

The way in which software is developed has changed considerably since the emergence of agile methods in the late 1990s [1], inspired by the Agile Manifesto [2]. In contrast to previously dominant classical methodologies, which presented problems concerning cost and deadlines, and other shortcomings [3], Agile Software Development (ASD), or simply agile methods, introduced new principles, methods and tools and have achieved prominence in the software industry for presenting more satisfactory results [4]. The ASD has attracted the interest of the academia, where research on this subject has obtained relevant representation in recent years [5].

Migration from classical development to agile methodologies takes time and effort. It has been focusing on software companies for a number of years, mainly because of the risk of wasted time and investment [6] and the obstacles typically encountered on this journey [7]. The adoption of ASD is an ongoing process in constant evolution and maturation, of all the team and company structures, including people, technologies, management and process. Therefore, it is not an end in itself, but an ongoing process of organizational learning [8].

© Springer International Publishing AG 2018
V. A. Santos et al. (Eds.): WBMA 2017, CCIS 802, pp. 21–30, 2018.
https://doi.org/10.1007/978-3-319-73673-0_2

Researchers have studied and developed new methods and tools to evaluate the processes that sustain the ASD, making it possible to measure the progress of its adoption, helping teams in the continuous improvement process and supporting the comparison of agility among teams and organizations [6]. However, there are still few models and methods of measurement proposed and, for the most part, still exposed to many problems and challenges [9]. Furthermore, these methods have generated discussions in the academic community about their alignment with the agile principles [6, 10] present in the Agile Manifesto, a common basis for agile methods.

The objective of this work was to analyze the main methods and tools of ASD evaluation in relation to the agile principles of flexibility, simplicity and pursuit for technical excellence, and to propose a solution more in line with these parameters.

Section 2 describes the research methodology used in this work. Section 3 mentions the main agile assessment tools and methods. Section 4 presents the preliminary results obtained so far. Finally, Sect. 5 concludes the discussions of this study and indicates future work.

2   Research Methodology

At the begin of the research were searched the following strings: "Agile AND Self-Assessment", "'Agile Software Development' AND Assessment", "Agile AND Assessment AND Process Improvement" AND "Agile AND (Practices OR Methods)" within the bases IEEE xplore, Springer, ACM, Elsevier Journal of Systems and Software and Google Scholar. In search of agile assessment methods and it characteristics and characteristics of agile practices. After, we selected the articles based on three criteria: first, if the article presents an assessment method. Second, if it summarizes or analyzes an assessment method. Third, if the article presents characteristics of agile practices that could be used to create the evaluation criteria for each practice in ASA.

Based on this, a literature review of 21 articles were read and then mapped the particular characteristics of each method. The mapping was built by checking specific characteristics. These characteristics were capacity of the method to be flexible to a team or organization context, the number of evaluation criteria, if it is a continuous improvement enabler and the method comprehensiveness. The characteristics were derived from the agile principles found in the Agile Manifesto.

So, a critical analysis was made related to the adherence of the assessment methods to the characteristics. The First analysis was if an assessment method is sensitive to a team or organization context what implies in greater or lesser flexibility. The Second analysis was if an assessment method has an increased or reduced number of evaluation criteria what implies in greater or lesser simplicity. The third analysis was if the method has or not an explicit feature that enables the assessor improve continually. Ultimately, not related with agile principles, the comprehensiveness of the method. It means how many practices and agile characteristics the assessment method covers. From the first three characteristics analyzed was possible to verify the alignment of the assessment methods with the agile principles of flexibility, simplicity and pursuit for excellence set out in the Agile Manifesto. Subsequently, from the issues in alignment between assessment methods and agile principles found. A new method and a prototype were proposed to enable better tuning in relation to the agile principles.

3   Main ASD Assessment Methods and Tools

As mentioned, the number of ASD models and assessment methods is relatively low. The works of Nafchi et al. [6] identified the main methods and evaluation tools of ASD published in recent years:

- Comparative Agility (CA) by William et al. [11]: A tool that measures the level of agility between teams or organizations through a 125-question questionnaire. The verified items address the agile practices present in SCRUM and XP and are answered using the Likert scale [12];
- OPP Framework by Soundararajan et al. [9]: the method considers three spheres for assessing agility, which are the adaptation of the method to agile principles, the company's ability to apply the method and the effectiveness of the method;
- Sidky Agile Measurement Index (SAMI) by Sidky et al. [13]: the tool consists of 4 components that are: agility levels; agile principles; agile practices; and indicators. The evaluation is based on the verification of 300 indicators that measure organizational and practical characteristics with an aim to achieve the implementation of agile principles;
- Thoughtworks Assessment Model (TAM) by the company Thoughtworks [14]: an online self-assessment tool consisting of 21 questions that when answered indicate the agility level of a team or agile organization;
- 4-D Framework (4-D) by Qumer and Henderson-Sellers [15]: self-assessment method based on 4 dimensions that are: scope of the method; agility characterization; characterization of agile values; and characterization of the software development process. The method has 23 questions related to these dimensions, resulting in the level of agility of a team or agile organization.

3.1   Analysis of ASD Main Methods and Assessment Tools

The inconsistencies between ASD assessment methods and agile principles may lead to a low interest in the application of these methods by practitioners [10]. That is the reason why the alignment between them is so important. At this stage of the work, the agile evaluation methods CA, SAMI, TAM, 4-D and OPP were analyzed critically, seeking to identify these possible misalignments. The following inconsistencies and considerations were raised upon completion of this preliminary analysis:

- **Inconsistency with the agile principle of flexibility:** As mentioned above CA is composed by a group of statements that indicates an organization agility level. These statements are related with agile practices and are not allowed to be chosen given a team or organization context. Could infer so, that if the assessor does not want to apply a particular practice he will be negatively impacted in his agility level. Similarly, as quoted SAMI has indicators, related with agile practices, that help an organization understand to what extent it is agile using five agility levels. The indicators measure agile characteristics within the organization through questions that try to check the presence of these agile characteristics. In this way, if a question is marked with a null response because is a practice not applicable within the organization. The assessment, which is the agility level, will be impaired. Even if the practice is misaligned with the organization context. The other methods OPP, 4-DAT and TAM presents a similar pattern as described in CA and SAMI. Considering that all the explained methods measures agility levels based on the presence of agile practices and more presence means a higher agility. In addition, the methods do not allow choose the practices or characteristics given a team or organization context. So, in this aspect, the models quoted is similar to that proposed by CMMI [16], since it evaluates the software development process based on maturity levels. The analogy between CMMI and Agile Assessment Methods is that one measures processes and the other practices and, the first is based on maturity level and the second in agility levels. Therefore, the evaluation models cited induce the evaluated team or organization to adopt practices that may not be appropriate to the context at that time in order to achieve higher levels of agility. Therefore, these five models are inconsistent with the agile principle of flexibility;

- **Inconsistency with the agile principle of simplicity:** the CA tool consists of 125 characteristics of agile methods, evaluated according to the Likert scale [12]. SAMI consists of 300 indicators that measures an organization agility level. Assuming that a team takes two minutes, on average, to evaluate a characteristic or indicator of the aforementioned methods, it would take around 4 h to respond to a complete assessment through CA and 10 h through SAMI. The principle of simplicity is described in the Agile Manifesto as the art of maximizing the amount of work that did not have to be done [2]. It was assumed that it is counter-intuitive to have such a large number of questions that demand such a considerable amount of time for its application. Thus, CA and SAMI are inconsistent with the agile principle of simplicity. The OPP method, which evaluates the agility of a team by means of 27 practices (i.e., criteria), was presented as the simplest among them;

- **Inconsistency with the agile principle of pursuit of excellence:** all tools analyzed, even in different ways, indicate the level of agility of a team after performing an evaluation, in other words they indicate the current situation. It is observed in these methods the absence of extensions that provide the establishment of goals and action plans that aim at the continuous improvement of the process of adoption of the agile methodology or its evolution in teams that have already implemented such an approach. Thus, it can be assumed that the agile principle of pursuit for excellence is not covered in its totality in the methods and tools analyzed;

- **Comprehensive agile evaluation methods and tools:** it was observed that the evaluation methods CA, SAMI and 4-D have been considered as only a perspective of the agile development process. The CA verifies the presence of agile practices that are inherent characteristics in the team or organization. SAMI measures an organizational characteristic related to a particular agile practice. The 4-D method verifies the presence of agile characteristics related to one of its 4 dimensions: scope of the method; agile characterization; characterization of agile values; characterization of the software process. On the other hand, the OPP method uses in its evaluation three perspectives: the adaptation of the method of development to the agile principles, the capacity of a team to use the method and the effectiveness of the method itself. The OPP method is apparently more comprehensive than the others evaluated.

4 Preliminary Results

4.1 The Agile Self-assessment Method

From the observation of the inconsistencies in alignment between the ASD assessment methods and tools and some principles originated in the Agile Manifesto [2], the Agile Self-Assessment (ASA) method was proposed. The ASA proposes to address these gaps by making evaluation criteria more flexible to the application context, simplifying the assessment and its ability to promote continuous improvement, and proposing comprehensive evaluation perspectives to the method. The main characteristics of ASA are described below:

- **Flexibility of the evaluation criteria to the application context:** the ASA method establishes evaluation criteria beforehand, also known as practice and the correspondent evaluation criteria for each practice. However, ASA allows agile practices that are not aligned with the context of the team or organization to be disregarded, and thus, only the practices that are aligned with the team or organization context are counted in the evaluation result. For example, the practice of pair programming is not always consensus in all agile teams, and it is possible to disregard this practice, as an evaluation criterion, because of the organization context is not aligned with it. This approach offers greater flexibility for the ASA, when compared to the other methods described in Sect. 2. In contrast, the option to remove the initial practices from the evaluation will require maturity and good sense from the teams, since they could disregard important agile components for an effective evaluation. In short, in ASA, agile teams will be allowed to choose the practices that are compatible with their context, what is not allowed in the other mentioned methods. Therefore, ASA have greater flexibility, when compared, with the other analyzed methods.
- **Simplicity in the application of the evaluation:** based on the analysis of the main methods of evaluation of the ASD, described in Sect. 3.1, it is noticed that the agile principle of simplicity is more aligned to the OPP method because it involves less evaluation criteria. Therefore, it was decided to adopt the evaluation items of this model as the initial basis for the ASA. These evaluation items are the objectives, principles and practices present on OPP. Also, the relationship chain between these evaluation items. In a complementary way, when examining the OPP, it was observed that it would be possible to merge four of its agile practices into only two, reducing the total of practices to 25 and consequentially the number of evaluation criteria correspondent to the merged practices. In the ASA, the practice "iterative and incremental development" and "small and frequent releases" has become just one practice, called "iterative and incremental development and small, frequent releases". The practice of "iterative and incremental development" is based on development through

evolutionary cycles of product functionalities over time and on staged deliveries of the software. The practice of "small and frequent releases" considers that delivery of development should be small and frequent, in an incremental way. Thus, it was possible to observe that the two practices could be merged because they intersect. Finally, the "automated test build" practice is described in the OPP as the automatic construction of a software after the commit of a developer and the automatic realization of the unit tests. However, the practice of "continuous delivery" includes in its scope the process of building and testing automated systems. It is noted that the practice "automated test build" is part of the "continuous delivery" practice, and could therefore be merged also. In this way, it was possible to reduce the number of evaluation criteria in ASA to 25 practices and 54 evaluation criteria related to these practices that support measurement of agile adoption. In comparison with CA and SAMI, ASA is simpler. Thus, more aligned with the simplicity agile principle;

- **Introduction of continuous improvement to the evaluation method:** the ASA method considers in its evaluation application approach the possibility of jointly implementing the continuous improvement of agility. For this, it uses the PDCA methodology, also known as Shewhart Cycle or Deming Cycle. The PDCA (Plan, Do, Check, Act) has as its basic function the aid in the diagnosis, analysis and prognosis of organizational problems, being extremely useful for solving problems and very effective in the search for continuous improvement [17]. After applying an agile assessment through the ASA, the team or organization outlines action plans and improvement goals on practices that are identified as still deficient based on the gap between the evaluation result for the current state of agile adoption and the target state, this is the Planning stage. The evaluation result is generated through the assessor application of ASA by the selection of present or absent evaluation criteria from the listed practices in ASA, columns "Current Evaluation" and "Target" shown in Fig. 2, and the result is presented for both, current state and target state, as shown in the Fig. 3. Soon after, the team executes the action plan defined jointly by the evaluated team: this is the Execution phase. Again, after a period of time defined by the team under evaluation, it is submitted to a new examination by the ASA method: this is the Verification step. As the new ASA assesses results, the team compares the improvement actions and planned goals at the beginning of the cycle, performs a critical analysis, considers new chances for improvement, and can make decisions about the next steps: this phase is called Action. After this, the cycle starts again with the Planning phase. It is expected that the PDCA cycle execution will bring about constant improvement of the ASD, making the evaluation method an instrument of improvement, not only a reflection of possible agility problems of the team. As criteria of analysis, were searched on the evaluation methods features that are enablers of continuous improvement. Although, the evaluation methods analyzed did not show these features. Therefore, these methods are less aligned with the pursuit for excellence agile principle. However, ASA was built with PDCA, continuous improvement methodology. Thus, ASA is more aligned with the pursuit for excellence agile principle than the other methods because it provides continuous improvement;

- **Comprehensive assessment dimensions:** the ASA method proposes to use the same evaluation dimensions suggested in the OPP, assessing, in addition to the suitability of software development to the agile principles, the capacity and effectiveness of a team or organization in that journey. This more comprehensive option considers the means and quality of the results achieved by a team or organization to what is required as satisfactory by the evaluation method, so it is presented as a more complete approach. Up to the present time of this research, efforts have focused on the development of the ASA method and prototype in the capacity assessment dimension to agile principles. The other dimensions will be considered in the future work.

4.2   The Agile Practices Assessment Criteria

The next step after mapping the agile practices that would make up the ASA method was to develop the criteria that would be used to assess the adoption of agile practices by teams or organizations.

The evaluation criteria for each of the 25 agile practices in ASA were based on a review of the literature. In addition to the literature review, the observable properties of people, projects and processes found in the OPP method were used as the basis for creating evaluation criteria for ASA. In ASA, on average, each practice has 3 criteria. Figure 1 presents the relationship between objectives, principles and practices as the criteria behind the practices. First, related to the relationship is possible to measure how aligned to the agile objectives and principles is a team or organization based on the adoption of the agile practices. Second, related to the practices is possible to measure the adoption of a practice based on the presence of related criteria.

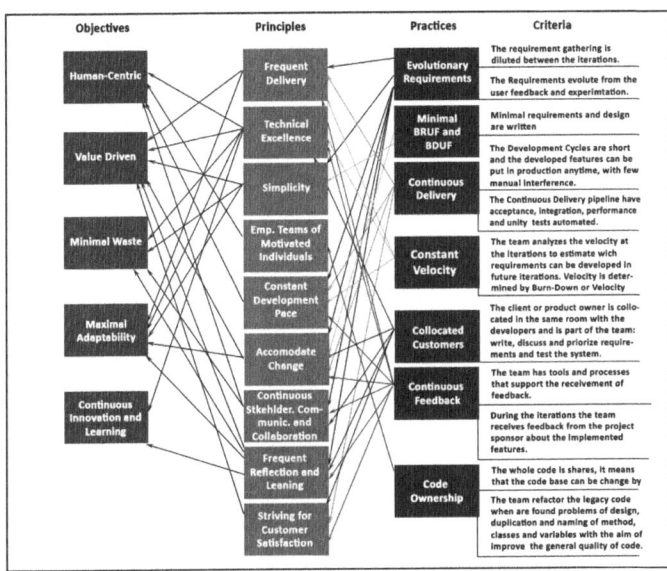

Fig. 1. Examples of relationships between objectives, principles, practices and ASA assessment criteria.

4.3   The Agile Self-assessment Tool Prototype

After selecting the agile practices, that would compose the ASA and the respective assessment criteria, a prototype was elaborated with the purpose of validating the proposal of this method. This prototype is presented in Fig. 2. In the leftmost part of Fig. 2 it is possible to observe the option of applying or not the agile practices in the assessment context. In the central part, the highlighted practices and their evaluation criteria are noted. For each criterion, to the left side of the prototype, it is informed the suitability or not of the team or organization in relation to the criteria. Note that there are two options to fill in on leftmost part of the prototype. Both are considered during the Verification cycle of the PDCA of ASA. The first, identified as "Current Evaluation", is used to evaluate the current situation of the team; the second, called "Target", is informed to set improvement goals for the next PDCA cycle and application of ASA.

Prototype: Agile Self-assessment

Practices

			Current Evaluation	**Target**
Does the practice apply?	**Evolutionary Requirements**		Does it have one? Yes/No. (Current)	Does it have one? Yes/No. (Target)
Yes	Criterion 1	The effort in surveying the requirements is diluted between the interactions.	No	Yes
	Criterion 2	Requirements evolve from user experimentation and feedback.	Yes	Yes
Does the practice apply?	**Code Refactoring**		Does it have one? Yes/No. (Current)	Does it have one? Yes/No. (Target)
Yes	Criterion 1	The architecture, design and code are refactored during the development of the system	Yes	Yes
	Criterion 2	The team keeps the code simple, commented, encapsulated, committed with common notation and without repeating code snippets. This maintenance is performed during interactions or at predefined times.	No	Yes

Fig. 2. Prototype for the ASA tool: evaluation criteria. See the full prototype in http://bit.ly/agile-self-assessment

Another feature implemented in the ASA prototype was the presentation of the evaluation result. As shown in Fig. 3, three ranges of team suitability values were used for agile practices: excellent (80–100%), good (40–79%) and poor (0–39%). And, following

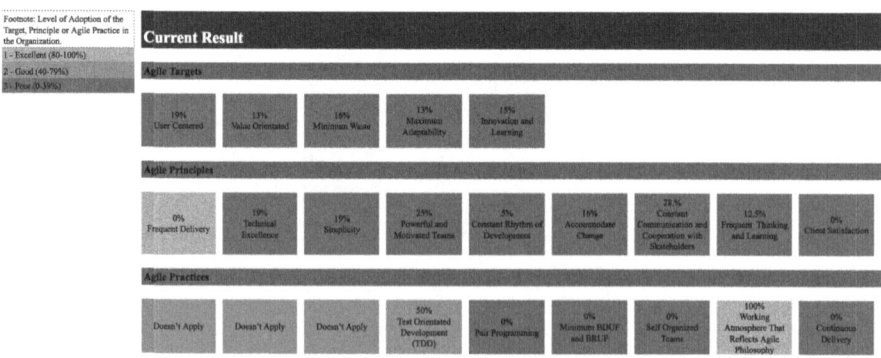

Fig. 3. Prototype for the ASA tool: evaluation result

the OPP proposal, the capacity results obtained from the practices are used to establish adherence to agile principles and, consequently, to agile objectives.

5 Preliminary Conclusions and Future Work

As already mentioned at the beginning of this paper, inconsistencies between ASD assessment methods and agile principles can lead to low interest in the application of these methods by practitioners. Currently, besides the fact that there are few methods and tools for this purpose, there are ongoing discussions in the academic community about the presence of inconsistencies in alignment with agile principles.

This work analyzed the main methods of evaluation of ASD and pointed out problems in relation to the agile principles of flexibility, simplicity and pursuit for excellence. From these gaps and the review of the literature, a new method - Agile Self-Assessment (ASA) was proposed. The ASA seeks to address these inconsistencies, in addition to providing a new aspect of evaluation, continuous improvement through PDCA cycles. A prototype was developed to apply the ASA method.

As a future work, the ASA tool should be applied in case studies in order to evaluate the real effectiveness of the method developed with development teams. The prototype will also be complemented with the dimensions of adequacy and effectiveness of the OPP method.

References

1. Dingsøyr, T., Nerur, S., Balijepally, V., Moe, N.B.: A decade of agile methodologies: towards explaining agile software development. J. Syst. Softw. **85**, 1213–1221 (2012)
2. Beck, K., Beedle, M., Van Bennekum, A., Cockburn, A., Cunningham, W., Fowler, M., Grenning, J., Highsmith, J., Hunt, A., Jeffries, R., Kern, J., Marick, B., Martin, R.C., Mellor, S., Schwaber, K., Sutherland, J., Thomas, D.: Agile Manifesto. http://agilemanifesto.org/
3. Johnson, J., Crear, J., Vianna, L., Mulder, T., Lynch, J.: Standish Group 2015 Chaos Report. http://blog.standishgroup.com/post/50
4. Fitzgerald, B., Stol, K.J.: Continuous software engineering: a roadmap and agenda. J. Syst. Softw. **123**, 176–189 (2017)
5. Al-Zewairi, M., Biltawi, M., Etaiwi, W., Shaout, A.: Agile software development methodologies: survey of surveys. J. Comput. Commun. **5**, 74–97 (2017)
6. Nafchi, M.Z., Zulzalil, H., Gandomani, T.J.: On the current agile assessment methods and approaches. In: 8th Malaysian Software Engineering Conference (MySEC), Langkawi, Malaysia, pp. 251–254. IEEE (2014)
7. Gandomani, T.J., Zulzalil, H., Ghani, A.A.A., Sultan, M.A.B., Nafchi, M.Z.: Obstacles in moving to agile software development methods; at a glance. J. Comput. Sci. **9**, 620–625 (2013)
8. Gandomani, T.J., Zulzalil, H., Ghani, A.A.A., Sultan, M.A.B.: Towards comprehensive and disciplined change management strategy in agile transformation process. Res. J. Appl. Sci. Eng. Technol. **6**, 2345–2351 (2013)
9. Soundararajan, S., Arthur, J.D., Balci, O.: A methodology for assessing agile software development methods. In: Agile Conference (AGILE), Dallas, TX, USA, pp. 51–54. IEEE (2012)

10. Fontana, R.M., Reinehr, S., Malucelli, A.: Maturing in agile: what is it about? In: Cantone, G., Marchesi, M. (eds.) XP 2014. LNBIP, vol. 179, pp. 94–109. Springer, Cham (2014). https://doi.org/10.1007/978-3-319-06862-6_7

11. Williams, L., Rubin, K., Cohn, M.: Driving process improvement via comparative agility assessment. In: 2010 Agile Conference, Nashville, TN, USA, pp. 3–10. IEEE (2010)

12. Likert, R., Roslow, S., Murphy, G.: A simple and reliable method of scoring the thurstone attitude scales. J. Soc. Psychol. 5, 228–238 (1934)

13. Sidky, A., Arthur, J., Bohner, S.: A disciplined approach to adopting agile practices: the agile adoption framework. Innov. Syst. Softw. Eng. 3, 203–216 (2007)

14. Thoughtworks: Thoughtworks Assessment Model. http://www.agileassessments.com/

15. Qumer, A., Henderson-Sellers, B.: An evaluation of the degree of agility in six agile methods and its applicability for method engineering. Inf. Softw. Technol. 50, 280–295 (2008)

16. Software Engineering Institute: CMMI for Development, Version 1.3 (2010)

17. Deming, E.: Out of the Crisis. MIT Press, Cambridge (1986)

Agile Testing in Brazil: A Systematic Mapping

João Farias[✉], Alexandre Vasconcelos[✉], and Ivaldir Junior[✉]

Universidade Federal de Pernambuco, Recife, PE 50670-901, Brazil
{jgfd,almv,ihfj}@cin.ufpe.br

Abstract. The increasing adoption of agile methodologies is changing the landscape of software testing. Both the manifold of testing techniques and the agile mindset have shown as challenges for professionals. In this context, this work conducted a systematic mapping of studies published in Brazil, with the goal of gathering evidence on the use of agile testing practices in the country. Using the Agile Testing Quadrants as classification model, testing techniques, their benefits and challenges were identified. This systematic mapping revealed that, despite the quality improvements and reduction of costs brought by the use of agile testing techniques, learning curves and lack of management cooperation introduce significant difficulties for the full adoption of agile testing.

Keywords: Software testing · Agile methodologies · Systematic mapping

1 Introduction

Given the exponential growth of human dependency upon software and the high risk associated with unexpected and incorrect behavior in computational systems, it is necessary to give prominence to testing processes in industry. The quality of testing activities is crucial for the success of software projects.

Traditional testing methodologies are focused on validating the software against a detailed and thorough set of requirements, ensuring that the expected product has been built. Conversely, agile methodologies recognize that is almost impossible to architect a whole project up front. Thus, in agile projects, testing is used to generate information about the product behavior, with the goal of driving the next steps to be taken. This paradigm demands from the professionals involved in software testing new skills and flexibility.

However, it is notorious the difficulty in adoption of testing in agile projects, due to issues related to technical capability, appropriated planning and skills to deal with changes. A survey promoted by SauceLabs [1] with 732 software professionals showed that 89% of them follow agile methodologies, but only 32% consider themselves totally immersed in the agile mindset. In the light of these problems and the importance of testing in software projects, this paper aims to obtain evidence of the application of agile testing techniques in Brazil. These evidences will provide an overview of studies of the field in the country and help researchers and practitioners to further improve their work in this context.

© Springer International Publishing AG 2018
V. A. Santos et al. (Eds.): WBMA 2017, CCIS 802, pp. 31–43, 2018.
https://doi.org/10.1007/978-3-319-73673-0_3

After this introductory section, Sect. 2 presents the theoretical references about testing and the agile movement. Section 3 explains the procedure used by this paper to search and select primary studies. Section 4 summarizes the findings of the research. Final considerations and suggested future works are exposed in Sect. 5.

2 Theoretical Background

This section explains the theoretical basis of this systematic mapping. Firstly, the origins and purpose of the agile movement are presented. Secondly, the definition of agile testing used throughout this study is detailed.

2.1 The Agile Movement

The experiences that led to the emergence of the agile development movement, which began in the 1990s, came as a reaction to traditional methodologies. These methodologies are focused on up front planning, static processes, dense documentation, and rigid requirements. In 2001, the Agile Manifesto [2] brought a set of 4 values and 12 practices for software development focused on customer interaction, valuing developers as thinking assets, flexibility for change and constant user feedback. These values and practices are rapidly being adopted by the software development practitioners and companies as a way to produce high quality products in short periods of time.

2.2 Software Testing

Software testing promotes the mechanisms to verify the behavior of a software product against a set of requirements, in order to mitigate the risks in its use. These activities, on average, represent 45% of the development costs of a product; additionally, inaccuracy in early failure detection increases the associated repair cost up to 100 times [3]. Thus, it is evident the importance of performing testing effectively and efficiently.

2.2.1 Agile Testing

Agile methodologies treat testing from a different perspective. Since agile projects are highly dynamic in nature and composed by short iterations, testing in these environments aims to provide information to drive planning for the following iterations and to increase the confidence of the development team in the value added by the product [4]. Crispin and Gregory developed, as an improvement to Marick's work [5], a classification model for the most commonly techniques for software testing in agile development projects, called Agile Testing Quadrants [6] (Fig. 1).

The model consists of four categories of tests with different objectives, divided by two axes. The Q1 and Q2 quadrants aim to support the development team in its activities, ensuring a better understanding of the product in development. Q1 quadrant encompasses the tests that drive the architecture design, validating its internal quality [11]. These tests give developers confidence that significant code changes do not cause functionality regressions [12]. Q2 quadrant consists of tests pertaining to requirements

Agile Testing Quadrants

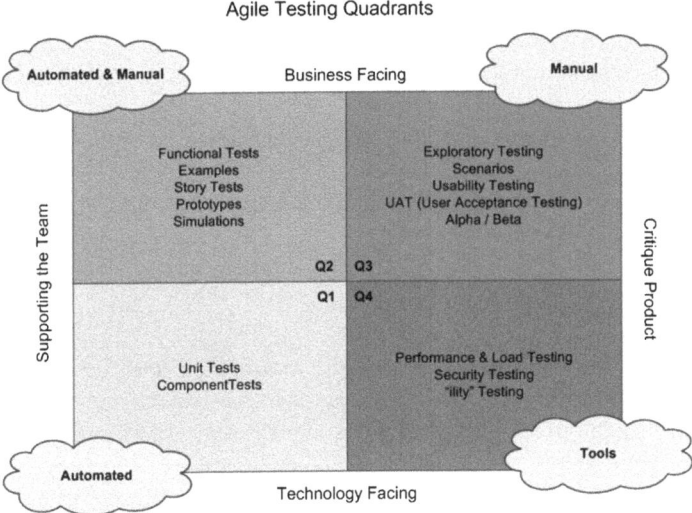

Fig. 1. Agile testing quadrants

design. Functional tests, generally automated, are performed in order to guarantee the system's external quality of the system. Prototyping, mock-ups, and wireframes help to validate whether the understanding of requirements is correct before functionality is implemented.

Tests of the Q3 and Q4 quadrants criticize the implemented product, with the goal of generating information to guide the progress of development. Q3 quadrant consists of tests which investigate if the product meets the user needs, using usability validations and exploratory testing. Q4 quadrant investigates the behavior of the system in production environment. Performance, load and stress tests validate if the system is able to withstand situations of extreme use. Security testing is critical to ensure that the product and the information it handles are protected from malicious attacks.

3 Research Method

The systematic mapping of the literature performed in this study followed the instructions of Kitchenham and Charters [7]. In the following sections, the steps covered during the research are distilled.

3.1 Research Questions

This study aims to answer the following Primary Research Question (PRQ):

- PRQ: How agile testing is conducted in Brazil?

The following Secondary Research Questions (SRQ) guide the process of systematic mapping of the literature:

- SRQ1: Which techniques related to the First Quadrant of Agile Testing (Q1) are used?
- SRQ2: Which techniques related to the Second Quadrant of Agile Testing (Q2) are used?
- SRQ3: Which techniques related to the Third Quadrant of Agile Testing (Q3) are used?
- SRQ4: Which techniques related to the Fourth Quadrant of Agile Testing (Q4) are used?

3.2   Search Strategy

Following the recommendations of Wohlin [8], a search was made based on the process of snowballing. However, given that this study is focused on the research carried out in Brazil, it was sought to identify researchers interested in agile testing working in the country.

From a list of researchers formed by literature indication [9] and manual inspection on conference proceedings, a search was conducted in the Lattes[1] curriculum system on April 16, 2017. For each curriculum analyzed, we selected the papers related to agile testing (published between 2012 and 2016) and the set of authors who collaborated in these works. The new list of researchers was analyzed by the same procedure. The process ended when no new researcher was identified. The process is described in Fig. 2.

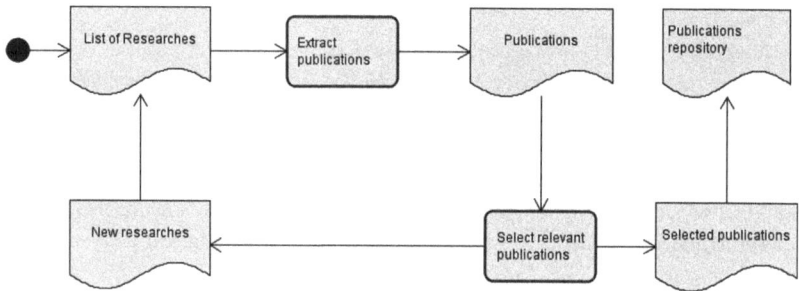

Fig. 2. Snowballing process

The process denominated "Extract publications" was supported by the tool Script-Lattes [10]. This tool aggregates publications of a set of Lattes curricula in a well-structured report, allowing the analysis of curricula in batch.

Using the ScriptLattes' report as input, the process denominated "Select relevant publications" was performed in three steps, using the inclusion and exclusion criteria from Sect. 3.3. Firstly, the report was analyzed in a semi-automatized way, utilizing a

---

[1] The "Lattes Curriculum" is considered the brazilian standard for information of scientific and academic production, students, professors, researches and professionals envolved in science and technology.

Python script[2] developed by the authors. This program asks the user if the title of a paper is relevant to the mapping, saving the paper's meta-data in a report when a positive answer is given. If the paper title was not determinant to exclusion of the search process, it was considered for further analysis. In the second step, the abstract of each paper was analyzed, filtering the studies which have shown non-conformity with the inclusion and exclusion criteria. Lastly, the remaining papers were analyzed in full text, excluding the papers that do not conform with the inclusion and exclusion criteria.

3.3 Inclusion and Exclusion Criteria

Table 1 lists the inclusion and exclusion criteria for primary studies. To be selected, a study must meet all the inclusion criteria and can not meet any of the exclusion criteria.

Table 1. Inclusion and exclusion criteria

Inclusion criteria	• Studies which exercise at least one Agile Testing technique • Studies with validation in industry; • Primary studies; • Peer-reviewed studies; • Complete studies published in periodicals or annals of congresses; • Qualitative or quantitative research;
Exclusion criteria	• Repeated studies, with no new information; • Chapters of books, artistic production, patents, abstracts, texts in newspapers or magazines; • Secondary or tertiary studies; • Studies limited to educational application; • Studies not available in UFPE's institutional network; • Studies not performed in Brazil;

3.4 Data Extraction and Synthesis

Information about primary study context, used techniques, and results were extracted in a standard form. The data was analyzed using scripts written in Python. Charts and tables were created using the LibreOffice tool.

3.5 Process Overview

The research was conducted in 3 stages. The initial list of authors was created using the list of researchers of agile methodologies in Brazil indicated by Goldman and Katayama [9], adding to a set of authors who published relevant (considering the criteria from Sect. 3.3) papers in the conferences SBES, SBQS, WAMPS, WASHES and WTDQS

---

[2] The Python script is available on the following link: https://goo.gl/PguSfd.

between 2012 and 2016. From this list of authors, the snowballing process described in Sect. 3.2 formed the studies repository of this mapping.

4   Results

4.1   Results of the Search Procedure

The snowballing process of authors resulted in the analysis of papers from 239 researchers, from which a total of 4664 unique studies were extracted. The analysis of titles and abstracts reduced the number of studies to 223. After the full text analysis, the final set of 40 studies was defined. Figure 3 shows the study numbers resulting from each step. The list of selected articles is available for download[3].

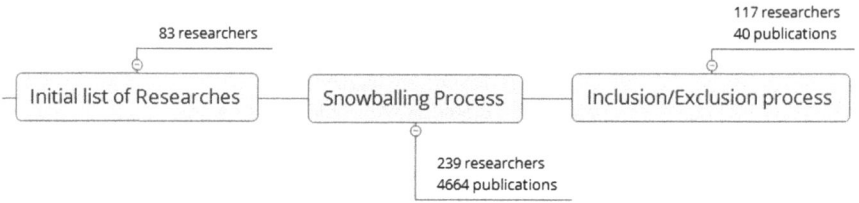

Fig. 3. Literature search results

Figure 4 shows the distribution of papers by year of publication. Of the 40 studies selected, 55% were published in the last 2 years, showing the growth of experiments with agile testing techniques in the Brazilian academic community.

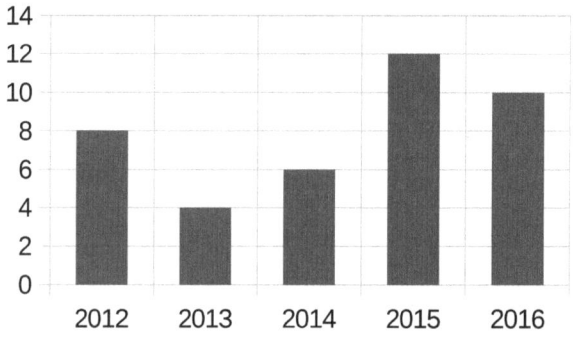

Fig. 4. Distribution of papers per year of publication

The primary publishing medium in these studies were conferences, symposia and workshops. The events with the highest number of publications were the Brazilian Software Quality Symposium (SBQS) and the Conference on Software Engineering and Knowledge Engineering (SEKE).

---

[3] List of articles available on the following link: https://goo.gl/19IAXO.

Figure 5 displays the paper distribution by related Agile Testing Quadrant. The most cited quadrants in the articles are related to development support (Q1 and Q2). Based on this, we can observe less interest in the study of techniques related to product critique (Q3 and Q4). Q3 is important to detect opportunities to improve user experience and validate whether the product meets the user needs. While Q4 is critical to guarantee the sustainability of software in the production environment, especially in times of intense use or under malicious attacks.

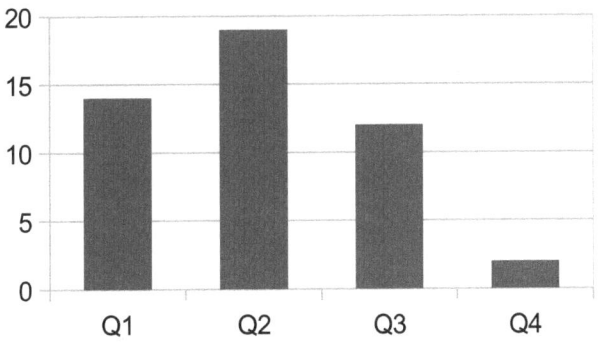

Fig. 5. Studies distribution per related Agile Testing Quadrant

The majority of the selected studies were the result of studies in the Northeast and North regions of Brazil, especially the states of Pernambuco and Amazonas, followed by the South and Southeast regions. The most active universities were UFAM, UFPE, UFCE and PUCRS. An important observation is that only 22 researchers (18% of the total) are connected to non-academic institutions, showing a possible lack of incentive

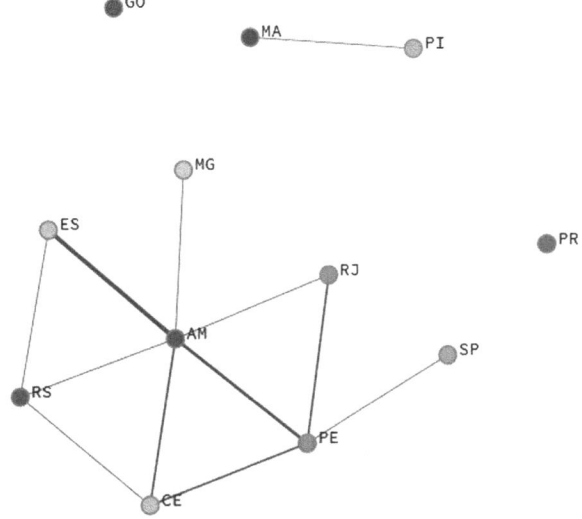

Fig. 6. Collaboration graph between researches of different states

to research and dissemination of experiences directly from the industry. Figure 6 displays the relationship of collaboration between researches of different states.

4.2 Evidences of Agile Testing Practices in Brazil

This section presents the results concerning each Secondary Research Question.

SRQ1: Which techniques related to the First Quadrant of Agile Testing (Q1) are used?

A total of 14 studies reported test techniques which support the development team with focus on code quality, as shown in Fig. 7. These studies demonstrated the use of 11 different techniques. The most used technique was Unit Testing, followed by Test-Driven Development (TDD) and Static Code Analysis.

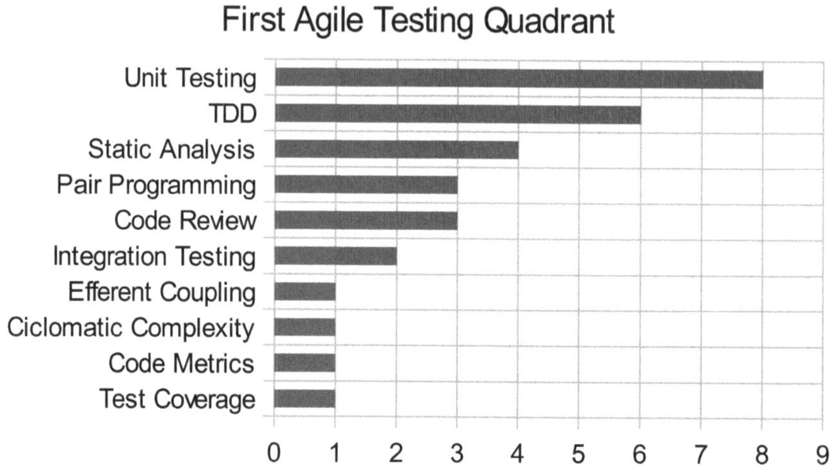

First Agile Testing Quadrant

Fig. 7. Techniques related to the First Agile Testing Quadrant

The work of Filho et al. [13] studied the impact of the TDD methodology in relation to the severity of errors detected after the building process. In projects that used TDD, only 27% of the errors found after building were considered severe. In projects that did not use TDD, 51% of these errors were considered severe.

Static analysis proved to be a good tool to ensure internal software quality [12], allowing teams to manage their technical debt and giving quick feedback on possible code degradation, such as code smells and high coupled components [15]. This software internal quality control enables teams to make changes without causing unexpected damages to the system, constantly adding value to the product [12].

SRQ2: Which techniques related to the Second Quadrant of Agile Testing (Q2) are used?

A total of 19 studies reported testing techniques aimed at supporting development with a focus on business, as shown in Fig. 8. These studies demonstrated the use of 5 different techniques. The most used techniques were Automated Functional Tests (AFT) and Usability Inspection.

Second Agile Testing Quadrant

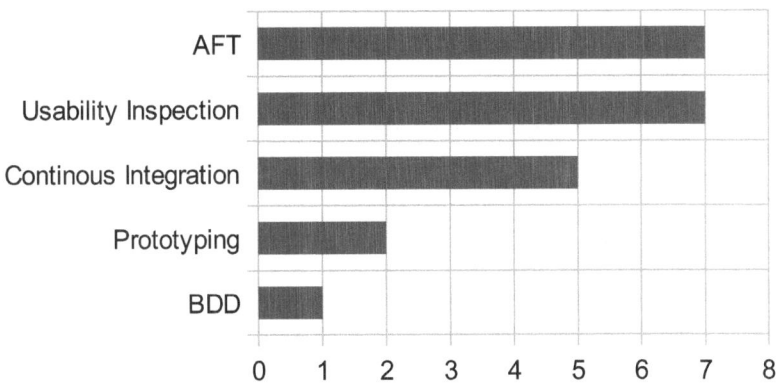

Fig. 8. Techniques related to the Second Agile Testing Quadrant

Due to the fast feedback and capacity to guarantee the external quality of the software, automated functional tests were shown as fundamental in agile projects. De Castro et al. [16] developed an abstraction of the Selenium framework for database verification which reduced the time of functional tests execution by 88% when compared to manual tests. AFT was also effective in contexts of mobile applications [17] and critical software [18].

The works of De Vaz et al. [19] and Rivero et al. [20] defined usability inspection procedures, demonstrating how this technique is able to detect failures in the requirements elicitation phase. The use of tools that aid the inspection process was effective, however, significant differences were observed in the quantity and severity of the defects when comparing inspectors of different levels of experience, reinforcing the need to value human skill in testing.

SRQ3: Which techniques related to the Third Quadrant of Agile Testing (Q3) are used?

A total of 12 studies reported testing techniques with the aim of criticizing the product with a focus on business, as shown in Fig. 9. These studies demonstrated the use of 4 different techniques. The most cited technique was Usability Testing.

The main objective of usability testing is to verify if the end user can use the product effectively and easily. The tester can rely on a list of usability principles [20], use tools for automatic fault detection [22, 23] and collect feedback from users in the form of surveys.

Falcao and Soares [24] used usability testing to validate competitive advantage a product. They analyzed whether a gesture-based device could bring effectiveness improvements to design professionals as compared to traditional mouse and keyboard-based input tools. After raising a list of usability issues, in addition to data on input error rate and effectiveness of use, the researchers showed that the device would not serve its users effectively.

Third Agile Testing Quadrants

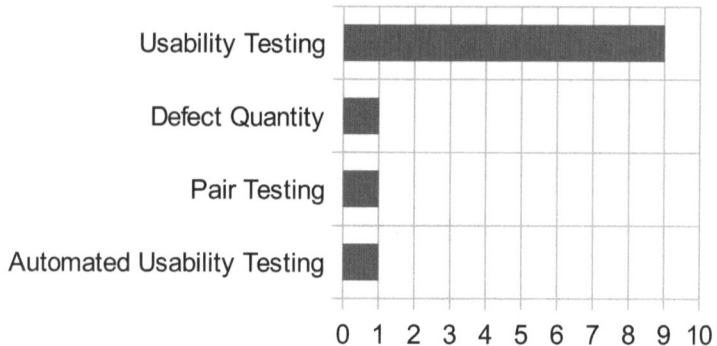

Fig. 9. Techniques related to the Third Agile Testing Quadrant

SRQ4: Which techniques related to the Fourth Quadrant of Agile Testing (Q4) are used?

A total of 3 studies reported testing techniques with the aim of criticizing the product with a technological focus, as shown in Fig. 10. These studies demonstrate the use of Performance Testing and Security Testing techniques.

Fourth Agile Testing Quadrant

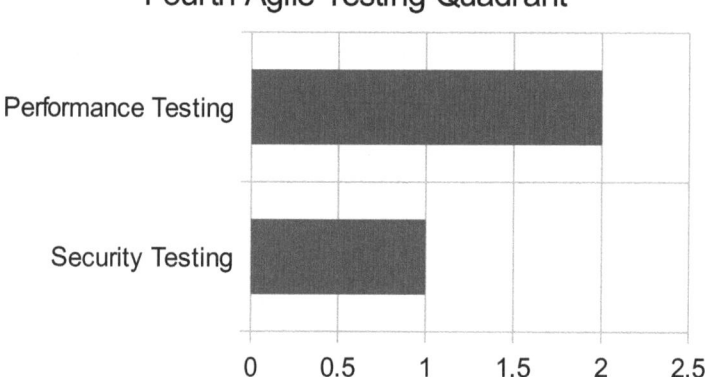

Fig. 10. Techniques related to the Fourth Agile Testing Quadrant

Tests from this quadrant evaluate the product under production conditions, where peaks of use and malicious attacks can lead to serious organizational damage. However, these tests, due their purely technical nature, are often postponed until the final stages of the projects [6]. Lucena and Tizzei [25] highlighted the problems caused by this type of decision:

> "When the software is finally deployed in the real customer environment one often finds integration and performance issues which could be prevented earlier. Late software deployments also limit useful feedback for the development team and delays customer return of the investment."

5   Final Considerations

This section summarizes the findings of this study and provide insights about the state of agile testing in Brazil.

5.1   Results

The frequency of techniques revealed by this study are similar to global surveys [1]. The Q1 quadrant tests proved to be able to increase the internal quality of the code, technically enabling programmers to incorporate the agile principle of "embrace change".

In agile projects, it is common that the requirements understanding becomes a problem, due to the inexhaustive documentation and rapid iterations. It was shown that techniques such as usability inspection and automated functional testing are able to mitigate this problem by ensuring that the correct product is being built.

The high number of papers reporting the use of usability testing can be justified by the fact that this technique is part of a set of user-centered design techniques. It was observed how the structured application of usability testing, especially when supported by tools, allows the detection of problems that seriously diminish the value brought by the software [22, 23].

Similar to Mohammed et al. [26], the studies related the Q4 quadrant have highlighted common problems of priority management. Due to their technical nature, security and performance issues are usually delayed until the end of the project. The problems detected at this stage are extremely costly and seriously reduce the value of the developed product.

5.2   Research Limitations

Approximately 12% of the papers selected by the snowballing process could not be analyzed in full text because they were not available for download in the UFPE's network. Possibly some relevant work was not included in the analysis.

Furthermore, this systematic mapping used only one source of information on the investigated researchers, named the Lattes Curriculum. Although Lattes is the standard for scientific research in Brazil, using it as the single source of information is twofold limiting. Firstly, the Lattes curriculum is primarily used for academic researches. The low number of non-academic papers discussed on Sect. 4.1 can be a result of this limitation. Second, it increases the likelihood of missing published works not included in researches' curriculum, specially for non-academic papers. Aggregating the Lattes results with other sources of information, such as ResearchGate, and direct contact with the researches would mitigate the risk of missing published papers related to agile testing.

5.3   Future Studies

The snowballing strategy presented in Sect. 3.2 was based on the work of Melo et al. [27]. We intend to validate quantitatively the effectiveness of this strategy in comparison with the technique presented by Wohlin [8].

The results of this systematic mapping will be used as source of information for the construction of a survey in practitioners, which will be conducted in the Porto Digital of the city of Recife. The goal is to compare the use of agile testing techniques in the Brazilian academic environment and the practitioners in this hub of development.

References

1. Sauce Labs: Testing Trends in 2017: A Survey of Software Professionals. https://saucelabs.com/news/sauce-labs-releases-third-annual-state-of-testing-survey-results. Accessed 5 June 2017
2. Agile Manifesto: Manifesto for Agile Software Development. http://www.agilemanifesto.org. Accessed 5 June 2017
3. Viana, V.: Um Método para Seleção de Testes de Regressão para Automação. Dissertação de Mestrado pelo Centro de Informática da UFPE (2006)
4. Williams, L., Cockburn, A.: Agile software development: it's about feedback and change. Computer 6, 39–46 (2003)
5. Marick, B.: Agile testing directions: tests and examples. http://www.exampler.com/old-blog/2003/08/21.1.html#agile-testing-project-1. Accessed 5 June 2017
6. Crispin, L., Gregory, J.: Agile Testing: A Practical Guide for Testers and Agile Teams, 1st edn. Addison-Wesley, Reading (2009)
7. Kitchenham, B.A., Charters, S.: Guidelines for performing systematic literature reviews in software engineering, vol. 2.3, EBSE-2007-01, Keele, UK (2007)
8. Wohlin, C.: Guidelines for snowballing in systematic literature studies and a replication in software engineering. In: 18th International Conference on Evaluation and Assessment in Software Engineering, pp. 1–10 (2014)
9. Goldman, A., Katayama, E.: Retrato da comunidade acadêmica de métodos ágeis no Brasil. In: Workshop Brasileiro de Métodos Ágeis. WBMA, pp. 1–10 (2011)
10. Mena-Chalco, J.P., Marcondes Jr., C.R.: ScriptLattes: an open-source knowledge extraction system from the Lattes platform. J. Brazilian Comput. Soc. 15(4), 31–39 (2009)
11. Beck, K.: Extreme Programming Explained: Embrace the Change, 1st edn. Addison-Wesley, Boston (2000)
12. Fowler, M.: Refactoring: Improving the Design of Existing Code, 1st edn. Addison-Wesley, Boston (1999)
13. Filho, M.C., Vasconcelo, J.L., Santos, W.B., Silva, I.F.: Um Estudo de Caso sobre o Aumento de Qualidade de Software em Projetos de Sistemas de Informação que Utilizam Test Driven Development. In: SBSI, pp. 315–326 (2012)
14. Gouveia, V., Júnior, N.L., Furtado, A.P., Junior, I.F., Furtado, F.: Avaliando as métricas ágeis utilizadas pelas empresas certificadas no nível F do MPS.Br. In: WAMPS, pp. 85–93. (2016)
15. Lucena, P., Tizzei, L.P.: Applying software craftsmanship practices to a scrum project: an experience report. In: WASHES, pp. 73–84 (2016)
16. De Castro, A.M.F.V., Macedo, G.A., Collins, E.F., Dias-Neto, A.C.: Extension of Selenium RC tool to perform automated testing with databases in web applications. In: AST, pp. 125–131 (2013)

17. Villanes, I.K., Costa, E.A.B., Dias-Neto, A.C.: Automated mobile testing as a service (AM-TaaS). In: SERVICES 2015, pp. 79–86 (2015)
18. Braz, A., Rubira, C.M.F., Vieira, M: Development of complex software with agile method. In: Agile Conference, pp. 97–101 (2015)
19. Vaz, V.T., Conte, T., Travassos, G.H.: Empirical Assessments of a tool to support Web usability inspection. CLEI Electron. J. **16**(3), 6–22 (2013)
20. Rivero, L., Kawakami, G., Conte, T.U.: Using a controlled experiment to evaluate usability inspection technologies for improving the quality of mobile web applications earlier in their design. In: SBES, pp. 161–170 (2014)
21. Neves, C.E., Campos, F.: Teste de Usabilidade do Módulo de Atendimento da Ferramenta Desktop de Gestão de Clínicas de Diagnóstivo por Imagem Uniclinika Ris. In: CONERG, pp. 117–135 (2014)
22. De, R.Q., Ribeiro, C.P., Monteiro, R., Marcio, M.: Análise de Usabilidade da Homepage de um Equipamento de Eletroencefalograma: Emotiv Epoc. In: ERGODESIGN, pp. 47–60 (2014)
23. Nascimento, I., Gaspar, W., Conte, T., Gadelha, B., Elaine, H.: Melhor prevenir do que remediar: Avaliando usabilidade e UX de software antes de levá-lo para a sala de aula. In: SBIE, pp. 806–815 (2016)
24. Falcao, C., Lemos, A.C., Soares, M.: Evaluation of natural user interface: a usability study based on the leap motion device. In: AHFE Conference, pp. 5490–5495 (2015)
25. Ali, S., Briand, L., Hemmati, H., Panesar-Walawege, R.: A systematic review of the application and empirical investigation of search-based test case generation. IEEE Trans. Softw. Eng. **5**, 1–22 (2008)
26. Mohammed, N.M., Niazi, M., Alshayeb, M., Mahmood, S.: Exploring software security approaches in software development lifecycle: a systematic mapping study. Comput. Stand. Interfaces **50**, 107–115 (2017)
27. Melo, C., Santos, V., Katayama, E., Corbucci, H., Prikladnicki, R., Goldman, A., Kon, F.: The evolution of agile software development in Brazil: education, research, and the state-of-the-practice. J. Braz. Comput. Soc. **19**(4), 523–552 (2013)

Metrics, Measurements and Mining Repositories in the Context of Agile

Using Function Points in Agile Projects: A Comparative Analysis Between Existing Approaches

Eduardo Garcia Wanderley[1]([✉]), Alexandre Vasconcelos[2], and Bruno Tenório Avila[2]

[1] IFPE – Instituto Federal de Educação, Ciência e Tecnologia, Garanhhuns, Pernambuco, Brazil
eduardo.wanderley@garanhuns.ifpe.edu.br
[2] UFPE – Universidade Federal de Pernambuco, Recife, Pernambuco, Brazil
amlv@cin.ufpe.br, brunotavila@gmail.com

Abstract. Agile Software Development has become increasingly common in the software development environment, but effort estimates in software projects using Agile methodologies are made differently from those made in traditional way projects. This paper presents a comparative analysis of the different approaches of applying Function Point Analysis (FPA) in software projects that make use of some existing agile methodologies. Through an experimental, empirical and controlled research, the existing proposals in the literature in order to test your application and analyze its results were evaluated. The results showed that in the context studied, the approach Agile Estimation Using Functional Metrics was best suited up.

Keywords: Effort estimation · Cost estimation · Size estimation · Agile
Scrum

1   Introduction

Agile methods are approaches for software development based on iterative and incremental development, direct involvement of customer, early delivery of higher business values and rapid responses to changes [1]. According to Soares [2], agile methods do not reject process and tools, documentation, contract negotiation or planning, but simply define them as secondary importance.

As reported by Mens and Demeyer [3], the companies' demand for products and services in the information technology field has been consistently increased, however the budgets and schedules are getting inflexible, due, for instance, to the need of cost-cutting policy and shorter deadlines for on time delivery performance. Therefore, the increase in quality and productivity becomes essential to software development. For this purpose, software metrics are used to: (i) serve as source of information to the monitoring of software process current situation; (ii) determine the evolution of software development; (iii) identify delays and deviations during project implementation; (v) prioritize accurate data over subjectivity and intuition.

Researcher's reviews have illustrated that in the last few decades, too little progress was made in the software estimation field [4]. This is a major concern in industry, because the low performance in estimation process very often leads to exceeded budget,

© Springer International Publishing AG 2018
V. A. Santos et al. (Eds.): WBMA 2017, CCIS 802, pp. 47–59, 2018.
https://doi.org/10.1007/978-3-319-73673-0_4

delays, sub-optimal allocated resources, contract losses or very low quality software [5]. Due to these problems, there is a high demand for enhancements in estimation process.

The development time of a feature in software can be measured by its size. However, there are several forms of measuring the size of software [6]. One of the best forms is the Automated Function Point (AFP) specification [7] which was standardized by the ISO/IEC 20.926 regulation [8] as a functional size measurement, added to the ISO/IEC 14.143 regulation [9]. A research from the Quality Assurance Institute [10] pointed that AFP is the proper metric to measure quality and productivity in software projects. In 1993, AFP became the most applied and studied metric in software engineering [11].

The advantages of using AFP are: (i) it is an objective method to find the score of an element; (ii) it might serve as a comparative basis between two different projects or even two different teams [12]; (iii) to equate communication and expectative about the system size; (iv) system size is defined by the customer insight [13]. Due to these circumstances, it is noticed that the use of AFP has become consolidated [14]. About 371 out of 893 of the licensed AFP professionals in the world are from Brazil [15].

In Brazil, many private and public institutions started using AFP on account of the several benefits this metric presents, and yet, by recommendation of regulatory agencies, it has been utilized in the contracts of development and maintenance of software in government organizations, which made AFP unanimous in the national metric industry [16]. In Brazilian public administration domain, normative instruction no. 4 [17], article 10 clearly outlines that the estimated financial cost must be measured. Article 14 affirms that the procedures planning and the measuring of the offered services – including metrics, indicators and values must be done.

Consequently, software development companies that already employ agile methodology must now have planning and measuring at top of agenda. Nonetheless, during agile development process, the software is incrementally developed, made in small iterations and the customers' feedback is an important asset to the following iterations. This implies that planning and estimation must be accomplished progressively [18]. Furthermore, taking into account the high number of iterations in agile methods, planning and estimation are done differently from classic software development [19]. From the perspective of estimation, All metrics and conventional life cycle models can be used in agile methods, but they require adaptation [20]. Therefore, specific techniques for agile methods were proposed and are being utilized in projects [1].

In this article a comparative analysis has been made between three different approaches (Extending Function Point Analysis [21], Function Point Analysis [22], and Functional Metrics [23]) to assess which was the ideal form of measuring effort in agile projects. The choices were mainly based on a systematic literature mapping. From this mapping, the three most relevant metrics were selected.

As a result of this work, it is noticed that two approaches can be satisfactorily used, and that a third one had been assessed truly insufficient and, therefore, may be discarded from all types of projects, not only the ones mentioned in this study. It is expected that the outcomes of this article may also support the using of effort metrics in agile methodology projects, benefiting mainstream software development community and, possessing a more accurate effort estimation, may bargain longer deadlines and better costs, assisting both customer and developer and, also, simplifying the adoption of AFP techniques by the companies that already make use of agile methods in their projects, leading the academic community to find new paths of research.

Due to the page break, some aspects of the experiment were suppressed. To obtain a more complete version, please contact us. This article is based on the master degree dissertation, presented by the main author, in 2015 [24].

2 Method

In software engineering, an experiment is a procedure carried out to combine facts with assumptions, speculations and beliefs so plentiful in software development [25]. It presents a systematic, disciplined and computable mode of assessment of human activity. Experiments are proper processes to achieve the validation of theories, confirm common knowledge, explore the relationships, assess model predictions or validate the measures. The possibilities of repetition, the full control over the process and the variables compose the major asset of the experiment.

The goals of an experiment study are the description, assessment, prediction, control and enhancement of products, processes, resources, models, theories etc. [26].

2.1 Experiment Planning

2.1.1 Goals
The GQM (Goal Question Metric) [26] approach was used to organize the objectives of this work, whose structure is presented as follows:

To assess the process of development effort estimation.

Intending to understand the utilization of different estimation processes.

In terms of accuracy and ease of application.

From the developers **point of view.**

In the context of the system analysts.

2.1.2 Metric and Question
What is the most accurate approach? Extending Function Point Analysis [21], Function Point Analysis and Cost Estimation in An Agile Development Environment [22] or Agile Estimation Using Functional Metrics [23]? The choices were given through a systematic literature mapping. From it, the three most relevant metrics were selected. The article about the non-selected approaches that were considered relevant, did not present suiT-able detailing about their right use, and for this reason, were disregarded. The criteria used to choose the best estimate was to elect the closest to the real value. For instance, if the real value was 50, the best estimate was the one that presented the closest value to 50. In order to appraise the accuracy of the experiment, the estimated value (measured in weekly function points) will be considered.

2.2   Experiment Description

2.2.1   Hypothesis

The main hypothesis of this study is the null hypothesis that says there are no significant statistic differences between the three approaches. Therefore, the work attempted to refute this hypothesis. The possible hypotheses are listed below:

- **Null hypothesis:** The estimated value (EV) is not significantly different when utilized the three distinct approaches.
- **Alternative hypothesis 1:** The estimated value is more accurate utilizing *Extending Function Point Analysis* approach.
- **Alternative hypothesis 2:** The estimated value is more accurate utilizing *Function Point Analysis and Cost Estimation in an Agile Development Environment* approach.
- **Alternative hypothesis 3:** The estimated value is more accurate utilizing *Agile Estimation Using Functional Metrics* approach.

2.2.2   Unity and Experimental Subject

The objects on which the experiment is based are called experimental units or experimental objects. Two studies from a municipal company were selected.

The person who applies the methods and techniques in the experimental unity is called experimental subject. This study employed eight system analysts who have never had contact with function points and development effort estimation.

2.2.3   Parameters and Factors

They are the input variables for the controlled experiment that defines the parameters (variables whose values will be kept constant throughout the experiment) and factors (Variables representing the procedures to be received by the experimental objects). They have as independent variables the measurement approaches and as dependent variables the estimated value. Since the analysts having different professional experience in estimation and the projects being distinct influence the experiment outcomes, non-experienced analysts were selected. To avoid interference in the experiment, the eight analysts were randomly arranged.

2.3   Execution Planning

2.3.1   Context

The experiment execution is part of the curriculum of the postgraduate student of Federal University of Pernambuco Informatics Center. The analyst team was preferred among the industry of Pernambuco state. All members are, at least, five years experienced system analysts.

2.3.2   Training and Participant Profile

Intending to standardize and ensure a minimum level of knowledge before the experiment performance, a few trainings were planned and performed earlier than the launch of the experiment pilot experiment scheme. The first training group was related to the function point technique. Firstly, they were introduced to the concepts and how to do the counting. After the conceptual starting point, exercises were practiced to assure that there was a proper understanding of the techniques use. Already knowing about function points, the participants had training in the experiment approaches. A total of 19 h were spent at the training sections, where 10 h were employed for function points whilst the approaches had been left with 3 h each.

Aiming to form cohesive and uniform teams, in which the effect related to the knowledge and experience could be mitigated, it was created and applied a characterization survey, where the participants could answer and be profiled.

2.4   Experiment Design

It is known that the proposed design for experimentation critically influences the formation of the teams. The Latin square was chosen as experimental model, due to its ideal suitability to the experiment. As stated in Juristo and Moreno [27], the Latin square presents as characteristic that each factor occurs once in each line and once in each column, it means that, it may take place only once to each possible combination of two blocking variables. For one to use the Latin square, it is necessary to set three different teams, where each of them will execute all approaches in each of the projects.

2.4.1   Round Execution and Pilot Scheme

With the purpose of systematizing data collection, some data (approaches/study, projects and analyst group) were divided into three groups, where two groups had three analysts each and one group had two of them. All groups executed the proposed activities and collected the data containing in the data collection form, to each one of the studies and with dissimilar tools.

A pilot stage was launched in order to validate the elements of instrumentalization and the data processing. At this stage, a fake project and different participants from the real experiment were used. At this point it was possible to diagnose the main issues and doubts the participants could have and, therefore, have them answered and not compromise the experiment performance.

2.4.2   Data Analysis Processing

In order to not interfere with the data analysis, approaches and analysts' info were omitted from data collection before data analysis.

2.5   Methods for Data Analysis

The analysis of the study aimed to compare the data collected from the experiment performance and check if the null hypothesis could be rejected. This analysis assessed the approaches utilized to estimate the software development effort in agile projects.

The performed experiment presented only one factor, and the distribution of the projects and approaches between the subjects were randomly made, by lot. With the purpose of rejecting null hypothesis, the ANOVA (analysis of variance) statistical model was utilized [29]. To assess the magnitude of these differences, it was chosen the Turkey's range test which is a single-step multiple comparison procedure and statistical test [30].

The ANOVA [29] statistical model says that in an experiment, each Y_{ij} observation may be decomposed as the following model equation:

$$Y_{ij} = \mu + \tau i + \in i_{ij} i = 1, \ldots, I e j = 1, \ldots, J$$

Where μ is the constant effect (general mean), τ_i is the effect of the *ith* procedure, ϵ_{ij} is the error related to the *ith* procedure in the *jth* experimental unit.

ANOVA is based on the partition of the total variance of response variable into components attribuTable to the procedures (variation among) and experimental error (variation within). This variation can be measured by the sum of squares defined to each of the components as presented in the following equations:

$$\sum_{i=1}^{n} (y_i - \bar{y})^2 = SST (\textbf{\textit{Sum of Squared Total}})$$

$$\sum_{i=1}^{n} (\hat{y}_i - \bar{y})^2 = SSR (\textbf{\textit{Sum of Squared Regression}})$$

$$\sum_{i=1}^{n} (y_i - \hat{y}_i)^2 = SSE (\textbf{\textit{Sum of Squared Error}})$$

Thereby, the equation is written: SST = SSR + SSE, in which the sum of squared totals is decomposed into the sum of squared regression and sum of squared error. This sum of squares is organized in a Table, named variance analysis Table (Table 2).

To test the H0 hypothesis (null), the F-test was used, as presented at Variance Analysis Table (Table 1).

Table 1. Variance analysis table.

Causes of variation	Degrees of freedom	Sum of squares	Median squares	F calculated
Procedures	I−1	SSR	MSR = SSR/(I−1)	MSR/MSE
Residual	I(J−1)	SSE	MSE = SSE/(I(J−1))	
Total	IJ−1	SST		

So whether F-calculated is higher than F-Tabled, then the null hypothesis (H0) must be rejected, it means that there are evidences of significant difference among at least one pair of treatment means, at α chosen level of significance. Otherwise, null hypothesis (H0) must not be rejected; it means that there are no significant differences between the treatments, at α chosen level of significance.

Consequently, the collected data will be assessed in order to try to reject the null hypothesis revealing that the mean of techniques are not equal, taking into account a certain significance level (α). At this experiment, regarding the small quantity of participants involved, there will be considered a 0,05 level of significance (α).

In other words, there will be adopted a 95% confidence interval on the outcomes of this study.

After concluding that there is significant differences among treatments by F-test, it was assessed the magnitude of these differences by utilizing a single-step multiple comparison procedure.

Tukey's range test allow one to test any contrast, always between two treatment means, it implies that it does not permit to compare groups with each other. The test is based on the Honest Significant Difference (HSD). The test statistic is given by the equation below:

$$TSD = q_\alpha(k, N - k)\sqrt{MSE/n}$$

Where q is the total studentized amplitude, Tabled, MSR is the mean square of residuals and n is the number of repetitions. The value of q depends on the number of treatments and residual degree of freedom. It was utilized a 5% level of significance. In case that the contrast is higher than Δ, the measures differ at α level of significance.

Since Tukey's test is somewhat independent from F-test, it is possible that, even with the value of F-calculated being significant, one may not find significant differences among the mean of contrasts [28].

3   Outcomes

The project/studies utilized at the experiment were chosen from a public company of Recife/PE, whose real values were selected without participants knowing. Thereafter, it were compared the estimations made by each one of them with real values, calculating the estimation error. The time necessary for colleting was not considered, because it was not an experiment concern. This fact gave participants freedom to spend the time they need.

3.1   Description of the Study

Previously than any outcome analysis it is necessary to present the characteristics of each study. These characteristics are:

- E1 study: New system with several features, developed in 3 iterations.
- E2 study: New feature for an ongoing system, with 2 iterations.

3.2   Collected Data

Listed below are the data collected from the participants. The Tables 2 and 3 illustrate the data divided into two studies. The first lines of each Table represent the estimation error value, presented in number of weeks. The value was obtained by subtracting the time estimated by each participant by the real time spent at the study development. The line 'means' reveals the mean of error of the approach. The line called 'general mean' illustrates the mean error value among the approaches. The line named 'effect' demonstrates the effect of every approach on response variable. The effect is calculated by subtracting the error mean of each approach by the general mean of the experiment. It is worth noting that the participant 8 did not deliver the data related to E1 study. Due to this fact, the E1 study remained with seven valid experiments.

Table 2. Experiment data with E1 study.

E1 study	CA approach	FM approach	EX approach
Participant 1	2,5875	0,1500	0,0309
Participant 2	2,5875	0,1125	0,2441
Participant 3	2,5875	0,6750	0,8333
Participant 4	1,2750	0,1875	0,3226
Participant 5	2,5875	0,4875	0,3844
Participant 6	1,2750	0,1125	0,0084
Participant 7	1,2750	0,6000	0,5025
Mean	2,0250	0,3321	0,3325
General Mean		0,8965	
Effect	1,1285	−0,5643	−0,5642

Table 3. Experiment data with E2 study.

E2 study	CA approach	FM approach	EX approach
Participant 1	1,5000	0,0750	0,3630
Participant 2	1,5000	0,0750	0,3630
Participant 3	1,5000	0,7875	0,7875
Participant 4	1,5000	0,2250	0,5020
Participant 5	1,5000	0,0750	0,4328
Participant 6	1,5000	0,4125	0,5896
Participant 7	1,5000	0,4125	0,5896
Participant 8	1,5000	0,0375	0,3806
Mean	1,5000	0,2625	0,5010
General Mean		0,7545	
Effect	0,7455	−0,4920	−0,2535

Tables 4 and 5 represent the errors (residuals) of each observation in relation to the error mean of each approach. These values illustrate the difference between the values obtained from each participant and the mean of each approach.

Table 4. Residuals related to each observation at E1 study.

E1 study	CA approach	FM approach	EX approach
Participant 1	0,5625	−0,1821	−0,3014
Participant 2	0,5625	−0,2196	−0,0882
Participant 3	0,5625	0,34286	0,5010
Participant 4	−0,7500	−0,1446	−0,0097
Participant 5	0,5625	0,1554	0,0521
Participant 6	−0,7500	−0,2196	−0,3239
Participant 7	−0,7500	0,2678	0,1702

Table 5. Residuals related to each observation at E2 study.

E2 study	CA approach	FM approach	EX approach
Participant 1	0,0000	−0,1875	−0,1380
Participant 2	0,0000	−0,1875	−0,1380
Participant 3	0,0000	0,5250	0,2865
Participant 4	0,0000	−0,0375	0,0010
Participant 5	0,0000	−0,1875	−0,0682
Participant 6	0,0000	0,1500	0,0886
Participant 7	0,0000	0,1500	0,0886
Participant 8	0,0000	−0,2250	−0,1204

3.3 Null Hypothesis

Considering that each study presents their own characteristics, it was not possible to group their outcomes in a single experiment, thus each of them was assessed as a separated experiment and due to this fact, the null hypothesis was rejected in each project.

The ANOVA statistical method was utilized as above-mentioned, and it states that one must compare the value of F-calculated with the value of F-Tabled, and whether F-calculated > F-Tabled then the null hypothesis must be rejected. The P1 project presents treatment and residual degrees of freedom (2 and 21 respectively). Consulting T-Student Table [30] with the values of F-Tabled $F_{(2,21)}$ will reveal the value of 3,467. At P2 project, the value of $F_{(2,18)}$ was used and the number found was 3,555. At Tables 6 and 7, the calculated value of F was always higher the Tabled value, and consequently the null hypothesis must be reject in all performed experiments.

Table 6. Analysis of variance data related to E1 study.

Causes of variance	Degrees of freedom	Sum of squares	Median squares	F-calculated
Treatments	2	13,3722	6,6861	
Residuals	18	3,8035	0,2113	
Total	20			31,6423

Table 7. Analysis of variance data related to E2 study.

Causes of variance	Degrees of freedom	Sum of squares	Median squares	F-calculated
Treatments	2	6,8967	3,4484	
Residuals	21	0,6331	0,0301	
Total	23			114,37

3.4 Tukey's Test

It was calculated an honest significant difference (HSD) to each project. Conforming to Tukey [30], if the difference between the means is higher than HSD one must reject the hypothesis of equality among the mean levels. According to Table 8, the HSD value of 0.63 in E1 study is higher than the differences among the means of each approach, and for this reason, the hypothesis of equality among the mean levels must not be rejected. In E2 study, presented at Table 9, it may be noticed that the HSD for this experiment was 0.22 and the means of the Extending Function Point Analysis (EX), Function Point Analysis and Cost Estimation in An Agile Development Environment (CA) and Agile Estimation Using Functional Metrics (FM) approaches were 1.5000, 0.2625 and 0.5010 respectively. Since the differences between all approaches were higher than HSD, one must reject the hypothesis of equality among the mean levels with a 95% level of significance. Seeing that the means represent the errors in estimates, one concludes that in E2 study the Function Point Analysis and Cost Estimation in An Agile Development Environment approach were found to have the ideal performance.

Table 8. The means values and the differences among them at E1 study.

E1 study	Mean	Dif. with CA	Dif. with FM	Dif. with EX
HSD	0,6300	N/A	N/A	N/A
CA approach	2,0250	N/A	1,6929	1,6925
FM approach	0,3321	−1,6929	N/A	−0,0004
Ex approach	0,3325	−1,6925	0,0004	N/A

Table 9. The means values and the differences among them at E2 study.

E2 study	Mean	Dif. with CA	Dif. with FM	Dif. with EX
HSD	0,2200	N/A	N/A	N/A
CA approach	1,5000	N/A	1,2375	0,9990
FM approach	0,2625	−1,2375	N/A	−0,2385
Ex approach	0,5010	−0,9990	0,2385	N/A

3.5 Outcome Assessment

As illustrated in Sect. 3.3, the null hypothesis was effortlessly rejected, what reveals that the approaches are different from each other. In every studies, the Function Point

Analysis and Cost Estimation in An Agile Development Environment – CA [26] approach presented very divergent numbers from other approaches and a high level of errors.

At E1 study, the Extending Function Point Analysis – EX and Agile Estimation Using Functional Metrics – FM approaches handed out very similar outcomes and a reduced error mean, and for that it may be concluded that in similar projects, both approaches can be considered acceptable.

At E2 study, the Agile Estimation Using Functional Metrics – FM approach was, considerably the ideal approach to measure projects with characteristics related to the study. This was largely due to a problem with the Extending Function Point Analysis – EX approach. It presents a statement that in new stories developed in iteration, only 53.52% of the activities can be developed in the same iteration, in other words, it becomes possible to conclude only up to 53.53% of the development of a new story. It leads the iterations that have only one story to low performance, since they become limited to the above-mentioned percentage, which is the case of E2 Study.

4   Concluding Remarks

From the controlled experiment results, it was noticed that the Function Point approach Analysis and Cost Estimation in an Agile Development Environment - CA is a very specific to the environment which the approach was described, since it determines fixed values of hours for each ALI found independent ALI found independent of the features that will be developed and because of this did not go well when it was used in an environment other than proposed by the author. It was also noticed that, despite the Extending Function Point Analysis - EX and Agile Estimation Using Functional Metrics - FM have similarities and values, the FM approach presented a lower mean error, especially with the E2 study and therefore was considered the most adequate for the study.

4.1   Threats to Validity

4.1.1   Internal Validity

At this experiment a few system analysts were utilized as subject and they may have suffered influence throughout the project and it may lead to some changes at the outcome. In relation to the subjects' commitment, they could have become discouraged during working time, although to bypass the problem it was accorded to their managements that they could earn a time off for their help in the project. The fatigue of estimating could have been another factor, and for this the delivery time was increased in 40% so they could relieve the pressure on the estimates delivery.

4.1.2   Conclusion Validity

It is about to the correctness of applying the statistical tests on the outcomes obtained during the experiment, and for this, a statistic professional monitored the project. At this study, the Tukey's Test was utilized to compare the outcome data.

4.1.3   Construct Validity

The training applied to the developers on the estimate metrics may not be fully understood by them, thus affecting the outcomes of the experiment.

4.1.4   External Validity

At this study, metrics to estimate software development effort using agile method were tested. In order to guarantee such validity, one may repeat the experiment in different groups with other characteristics in consideration of ensure the outcomes can be generalized.

4.1.5   Empirical Reliability

The procedures for carrying out the research were documented in detail, seeking to serve as a source of information and so, to enable that other researchers can repeat it in the future, contributing to a greater empirical reliability.

4.2   Future Works

The following works are recommended:

- Develop case studies about the theme involving Brazilian software development companies;
- Develop action researches for testing if the outcomes of this experiment may be confirmed by using them with other companies.

References

1. Sommerville, I.: Engenharia de Software. Editora Addison-Wesley (2011)
2. dos Santos Soares, M.: Comparação entre Metodologias Ágeis e Tradicionais para o Desenvolvimento de Software. Unipac-Universidade Presidente Antônio Carlos (2010)
3. Mens, T., Demeyer, S.: Future trends in software evolution metrics. In: Proceedings of the 4th International Workshop on Principles of Software Evolution, IWPSE 2001, pp. 83–86 (2001)
4. França, L.P.A., et al.: Medição de Software para Pequenas Empresas: uma Solução Baseada na Web. PUC-RJ, Rio de Janeiro (1998)
5. Usman, M., et al.: Effort estimation in agile software development: A systematic literature review. In: Proceedings of the 10th International Conference on Predictive Models in Software Engineering, pp. 82–91. ACM (2014)
6. Kan, S.: Metrics and Models in Software Quality Engineering. Addison-Wesley, Boston (2002)
7. Albrecht, A.J.: Measuring application development productivity. In: Proceedings of the IBM Applications Development Symposium, p. 83. GUIDE, IBM Corp., Monterey (1979)
8. SO/IEC 20926: Disponível em (2002). www.iso.org/iso/cataloguedetail.htm
9. Dekkers, C.: Measuring the logical or function a Size of Software Projects and Software Application. Spotlight Software, ISO Bulletin, May 2003
10. Perry, W.E.: The best measures for measuring data processing quality and productivity. Quality Assurance Institute Technical Report (1986)

11. Jones, C.: Function points. Computer **27**(8), 66–67 (1994)
12. Santana, C., Gusmão, C.: Uso de Análise de Pontos de Funções em Ambientes Ágeis. In: Engenharia de Software Magazine, pp. 33–40, 20 December 2009
13. Oest, C.: Quando a Análise de Pontos de Função se Torna um Método Ágil? In: 2nd Conferência Brasileira de Medição e Analise de Software, São Paulo, Brasil 2011
14. BFPUG: Brazilian Function Point Users Group, Número de CFPS por País (2008)
15. SISP: Roteiro de Métricas de Software do SISP: V. 2.0. Ministério do Planejamento, Orçamento e Gestão: Secretaria de Logistica e Tecnologia da Informação, Brasília (2012)
16. Governo Federal: Disponível em (2008). http://www.governoeletronico.gov.br/anexos/instrucao-normativa-n-04
17. Usman, M., et al.: Effort estimation in Agile Software Development: A systematic literature review. In: Proceedings of the 10th International Conference on Predictive Models in Software Engineering, pp. 82–91. ACM (2014)
18. Cohn, M.: Agile Estimation and Planning. Addison-Wesley, Upper Saddle River (2005)
19. Schmietendorf, A., et al.: Effort estimation for agile software development projects. In: 5th Software Measurement European Forum (2008)
20. Fuqua, A.M.: Using function points in XP - considerations. In: Marchesi, M., Succi, G. (eds.) XP 2003. LNCS, vol. 2675, pp. 340–342. Springer, Heidelberg (2003). https://doi.org/10.1007/3-540-44870-5_46
21. Banerjee, A.U., et al.: Estimating agile iterations by extending function point analysis. In: WORLDCOMP 2012 (2012)
22. Alexander, A.J.: Case Study: Function Point Analysis and Cost Estimation in An Agile Development Environment (2011)
23. Cagley, T.: Agile Estimation Using Functional Metrics. The IFPUG Guide to IT and Software Measurement IFPUG. CRC Press (2009)
24. Wanderley, E.G.: Aplicação de Pontos por Função em Projetos que Usam Métodos. Dissertação de Mestrado UFPE (2015)
25. Kitchenham, B., et al.: Towards a framework for software measurement validation. IEEE Trans. Softw. Eng. **21**(12), 929–943 (1995)
26. Sousa, K., De, D., et al.: Uso do GQM para avaliar implantação de processo de manutenção de software. Universidade Católica de Brasília (2005)
27. Juristo, N., Moreno, A.M.: Basics of Software Engineering Experimentation. Springer, Heidelberg (2010). https://doi.org/10.1007/978-1-4757-3304-4
28. Travassos, G.H., et al.: Introdução à Engenharia de Software Experimental (2002)
29. Fisher, R.A.: Statistical Methods for Research Workers. Oliver & Boyd, Edinburgh (1925)
30. Tukey, J.W.: Exploratory Data Analysis. Addison-Wesley, Reading (1977)

Adoption of Agile/Lean

Agile in 3D: Agility in the Animation Studio

Avelino F. Gomes Filho[1(✉)], Danilo Alencar[2], and Rodrigo de Toledo[3]

[1] Postgraduate Program in Computer Science (PPGI),
Federal University of Rio de Janeiro (UFRJ), Rio de Janeiro, Brazil
avelino.filho@ppgi.ufrj.br
[2] Knowledge 21 (K21), Rio de Janeiro, Brazil
danilo@k21.com.br
[3] Department of Computer Science (DCC),
Federal University of Rio de Janeiro (UFRJ), Rio de Janeiro, Brazil
rtoledo@dcc.ufrj.br

Abstract. Agile Software Development has been gaining importance because of its adaptability, focus on people, continuous improvement, and short construction and delivery cycles. Companies outside the software engineering context also desire such qualities. This paper presents a case study where a 3D animation production company adapted Scrum and Lean Kanban methods to achieve better results by reducing the effort required to create their products and make them available. The results demonstrate that the adaptation led to a shorter animation development time, helped the team track product evolution, increased automation, made the development process transparent and improved team engagement. This paper provides evidence that the animation industry can benefit from adapting and adopting Agile.

Keywords: Agile · Scrum · Lean · Kanban · Animation · 3D Studio

1 Introduction

Animation studios are companies that deliver solutions ranging from the creation of illustrations and small special effects to the development of feature films. They operate in creative environments, characterized by the non-linearity of their actions and by their complexity and even chaos. However, they also face the restrictions of corporate environments, such as costs, deadlines, scopes, client relationships, contracts, etc. [12].

The challenge of conciliating these characteristics, and the difficulty of making the professionals respect these restrictions and stop missing deadlines, led the 3D animation studio described in this paper to search for a solution to the following problem: How to do creative work while respecting the deadlines and the production pace agreed upon with the clients?

This work presents the result of the action research carried out and describes how Scrum and Lean Kanban practices were used to shed light on the problem

© Springer International Publishing AG 2018
V. A. Santos et al. (Eds.): WBMA 2017, CCIS 802, pp. 63–76, 2018.
https://doi.org/10.1007/978-3-319-73673-0_5

and help find a solution. The objective was to explore how Agile software development methods can be adapted to the production of 3D animation, engaging people not only in the development, but also in the self-management of their products, reducing delays and consequently improving client satisfaction. Here we describe how the work process was built collaboratively and iteratively by collecting efficiency metrics, feedback and views from those involved in the process.

The paper is divided as follows: Sect. 2 presents related work used as support for this study. Section 3 describes the action research method used. Section 4 presents the experiments carried out to build the management model used in the animation studio. Section 5 presents the results obtained in the study. Section 6 concludes this work and indicates next steps in the research.

2   Related Work

Agile Methods have crossed the boundaries of software development. They are currently used for teaching [6], scientific research [9] and hardware product building [4]. Animation and visual effect creation has also experienced the benefits of these methodologies. Yothino et al. [13] described the experience of adopting Scrum for visual effect production. The authors identify the framework's ability to increase control over the creation process and improve project quality as the main reason to adopt it.

In another application, the same group of researchers applied Scrum again, this time as a knowledge equalizer, so that professionals from different backgrounds could create visual effects collaboratively. The framework was used to speed up the creation process, in the short space of just three weeks [14].

These contributions show that Agile Methods can assist in the management of animation creation through iteration cycles. However, they were applied to new projects and controlled environments. The present research was applied to a real company, with the corporate pressures of costs and deadlines, and to an ongoing project. The goal was to reduce delays, identify bottlenecks in the process, and adapt not only Scrum [11], but Lean Kanban as well [1].

3   Research Method

The action research method was considered the most appropriate because of the need for researchers and study participants to collaborate, the qualitative nature of the results, the complexity of the system assessed, and the need to perform multiple experiment cycles to reach the best possible result [8].

This scientific method has similarities with Scrum [11] and Lean Startup [10] Agile development cycle. The researchers start by identifying solution hypotheses, plan the validation and execute the experiment. At the end, after result collection and analysis, the researchers can assess and propose new solutions to the problem, thus achieving continuous improvement [7].

However, there are challenges to action research, because data capture and analysis depends on qualitative information perceived by the researchers and obtained through feedback and interviews with the team under study. To reduce this challenge, we used the Cognitive Task Analysis (CTA) method. This method is recommended when the tasks to be analyzed require intense cognitive activity by the user, such as decision making, problem solving, memory, etc. [5].

3.1   Method

The activities carried out in this study began with an interview with the animator responsible for the team and the researchers. The purpose of the interview was only to identify the challenges faced by the production company.

Following the CTA process, based on the interviewee's information, a timeline with the most significant events the team had gone through was drawn. We then determined the most relevant points in the discussion. This way, we were able to classify the attention points into four types: Management, Development Process, Deadline, and Client. Figure 1 presents the result of this initial analysis.

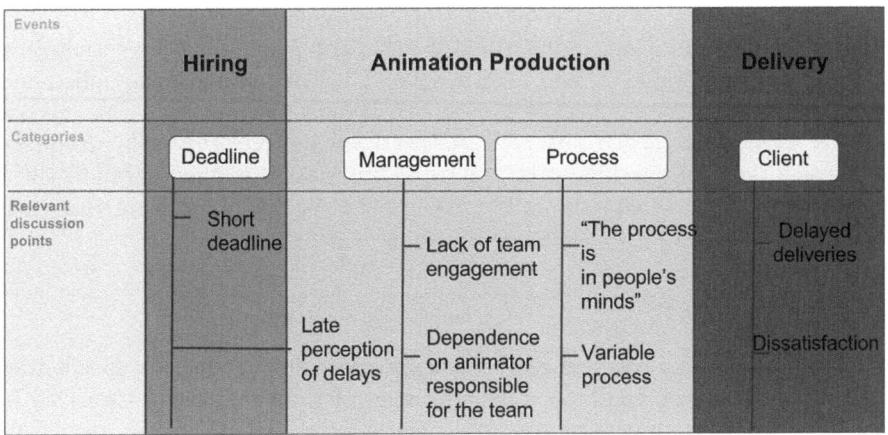

Fig. 1. CTA of information captured during the interview with the professional in charge of the animation.

Once classified, the issues were prioritized by the interviewee as follows: 1. "The process is in people's minds"; 2. The team lacks engagement with management; 3. Dependence on animator responsible for the team; and 4. Late perception of delays. According to the interviewee, variable process and client dissatisfaction are consequences of the prioritized problems. The short, one-week deadline is a given that cannot be negotiated.

This way we were able to understand the issues the company was facing, develop the research question (Sect. 1), and create assumptions and experiments to solve the problem (Sect. 4).

After applying the CTA, we carried out bibliographic research to assess how other organizations operating in a similar context have dealt with the issues identified.

Table 1. Experiment summary table

Experiment cycle	Problem	Objective	Duration
1st	Chaotic and unstructured process and high dependence on the responsible animator	To structure the work process	15 days
2nd	Delays and Process Variability	Define and give transparency to the process stages, highlight bottlenecks, increase team engagement	15 days
3rd	Delays and Process Variability	Deliver an episode of the animation in 7 days	15 days

We used the IEEE, Springer, ACM DL and Google Scholar databases to locate academic contributions. The most relevant results are mentioned in Sect. 2. Because the number of academic contributions was small, the researchers searched Google for industry solutions to this type of challenge.

Based on the obtained results, the researchers proposed a process-monitoring model based on Scrum [11] and Lean Kanban [1]. The method was applied and improved in three research cycles, each one lasting two weeks. At the end, a new interview was carried out with the head animator to record his feedback and assess the results achieved by the model in relation to the issues identified through the CTA. Table 1 shows the experiment cycles, the problem that each experiment tried to solve, goals and duration.

3.2 Limitations

The proposed model was created to accommodate the production specificities described in Subsect. 4.1. Some characteristics of the professionals involved in this experiment made the model implementation easier. The most important of these are the company culture of innovation and experimentation and the adaptation capacity of the team members.

Moreover, the results obtained are qualitative, so they depend on the subjective analysis by those involved both in the team under study and the research team.

Another limitation is the small number of academic contributions available on the theme. This limitation makes it difficult to compare the proposed model's results with others. The expectation is that this model can be adapted and applied to other producers, so we can assess its potential generalization.

4   Experimentation Cycles

4.1   Context

The company that participated in the action research is a 3D and 2D animation producer. It has several production contracts and provides services from scriptwriting to post-production. The team that participated in this research is composed of five people: two animators and a production assistant who work exclusively in the production under study, as well as a scriptwriter who is responsible for each episode's narrative, and a voice talent who does the character voices. The two latter team members divide their time among various animation teams.

The company's need to improve the way it manages its creative process arose from a new contract, whereby they would produce and publicize a series of two-minute videos published on YouTube every week. Production started in a poorly organized and hurried manner. The production stages started to get behind schedule, and team members missed what had to be done. It was important for them to visualize what was happening and how they could make up for lost time [3].

The challenge was how to efficiently manage the creation process for this animation series so that there were no delays, ensuring client satisfaction and a lasting contract. The initial delay was of more than seven days.

4.2   First Cycle: Scrum Adaptation

The first experiment cycle had the goal of making the creation process management easier. Because Scrum [11] is a simple framework with clearly defined development stages, roles and ceremonies, it was the method of choice for this goal.

During the cycle, items were defined that could make activity monitoring easier. The stories that represent the client's needs (User Story) were adapted to represent the series episodes. Each episode is defined by the producer's manager, who played the role of Product Owner (PO). His main responsibility is to define and prioritize the themes each episode should cover. He actively participates in each episode's planning and review when these are presented by the creation team. The professional in charge of the animation team played the role of Scrum Master (SM), facilitating the team's work. The remaining team members played the role of the Creation Team.

One of the assumptions for the animation series was that it would include recent topics in the media and promotions, so the PO must keep a clean Product Backlog. He has stories for one or two iterations (Sprints), which last two and a half weeks.

Iteration Planning (Sprint Planning) is done between the PO, the SM and the Creation Team. In this planning, the PO presents the episode topics and the team chooses what will be done in that iteration. For each iteration, three episodes are chosen to be part of the Sprint Backlog.

The team also adopted as Definition of Ready that the topic must have been chosen by the PO and debated with the team during planning. The execution is monitored through Daily Meetings. The episode is ready (Definition of Done) when it is created, rendered, edited and has the promotional material prepared.

At the end of the iteration, the revision meeting is held to show the animation to the PO and collect his feedback. The PO, the SM and the Creation Team are present in the meeting.

After the review, in the Retrospective Meeting, the team's feedback is collected about the method and how it could be improved. According to the team, Scrum was useful to define roles and significantly reduce the team's dependence on the head animator. That was important to "take people's minds off the process". However, the project started behind schedule, with stories that had not been delivered at the end of the iteration. The team also showed little engagement with project monitoring, and the process continued to be non-predictive, with tasks arising during the Sprint. Moreover, although they had realized that they were going to be delayed, they thought this was not very clear. In fact, the delay observed before the beginning of the experiment was not shortened.

4.3   Second Cycle: Life Cycle with Kanban

The objective of the second cycle was to make the process stages more transparent and the delays easier to visualize. Kanban was chosen because it is a method that can represent the entire value chain of the work process and reveal handoffs and bottlenecks [1].

The concepts adapted from Scrum were maintained: the roles of PO, SM and Team; the Planning, Daily, Review and Retrospective meetings; the definitions of Prepared and Ready; the Sprint Backlog; and the episodes as User Stories. After analyzing the activities carried out by the Team, it was observed that the creation of episodes could have been better described through the following value chain:

1. **Script:** Creation of the story to be told in the episode;
2. **Narration:** The voice talent reads the script;
3. **Modeling:** Creation of the animation items: characters, vehicles, objects, background, etc.;
4. **Blocking:** Animation of key sketches of characters and objects in the scene;
5. **Cleaning:** First refinement after blocking;
6. **Lip Sync:** Synchronizing the characters' movements and the narration;
7. **Refining:** Refinement of the animation to check for problems;
8. **Rendering:** Animation rendering, which results in the first version of the video, still without the background;
9. **Correction:** After putting the video together and rendering it for the first time, motions and element synchrony must be corrected;
10. **Composition:** Addition of background scenery to characters and objects;
11. **Editing:** The whole video is watched and, if needed, edited to fix any remaining problems.

Moreover, the need for the team to also focus on the promotion process of the episodes was identified. This process begins after the Blocking stage and involves composing the promotional material and creating the opening sequence that will be used to promote the animation.

Based on this feedback, the board was redesigned, as shown in Fig. 2.

Not all process stages are sequential. As can be seen in Figs. 2 and 3, after the Script is defined, the Narration and Modeling stages can be done in parallel.

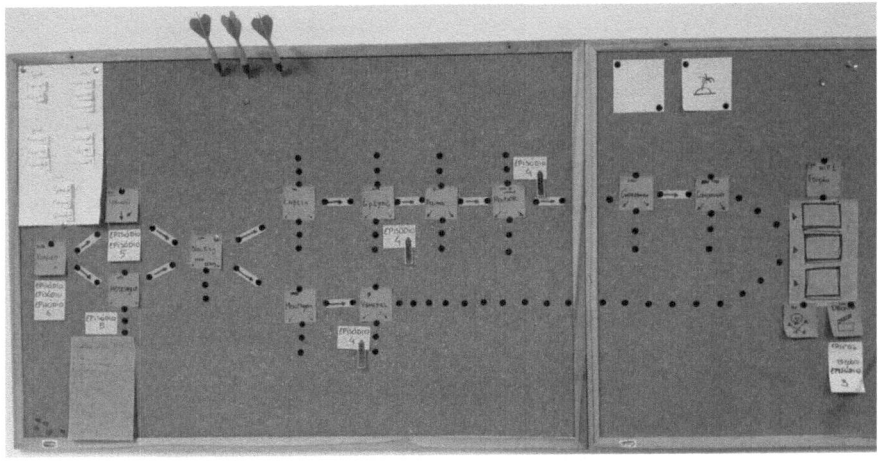

Fig. 2. Kanban Board to monitor animation production.

However, both must be ready for the Blocking stage. After that, the process is divided into two well-defined sub-processes: episode Creation (upper line) and Promotion (lower line).

Besides the board, the team adopted important Lean Kanban features: the first is a limited quantity of items in execution (Work in Progress). Each stage can have one execution item at most. However, because there are two animators on the team and each episode is two minutes long, they decided to divide the episode into Minute 1 and Minute 2, working on Cleaning, Lip Sync, Refining and Rendering in parallel. Minute 1 is placed above the name of the stage, and Minute 2 is placed below.

The action and waiting steps in each stage are also represented. When the episode is to the left of the division (three tacks), it means that the item is stopped, awaiting execution (To Do). When it is to the right of the tacks, it means that the item is being executed (Doing). When the animator concludes that stage, he moves it to the To Do column of the next stage.

Observing Fig. 4, the board should be read as follows. For the current iteration, Episode 4 was selected. Minute 1 of the episode is being rendered. Minute 2 is in the Lip Sync stage. Meanwhile, in the Promotion process, the composition was done and the episode is awaiting the opening sequence.

The Definition of Ready adopted by the team was maintained, but it started to be visually represented on the board by the three editing boxes (blue paper in Fig. 5). The first box is occupied by Minute 1, the second by Minute 2, and the third by the promotional material. When all three are completed, it means that the episode is ready.

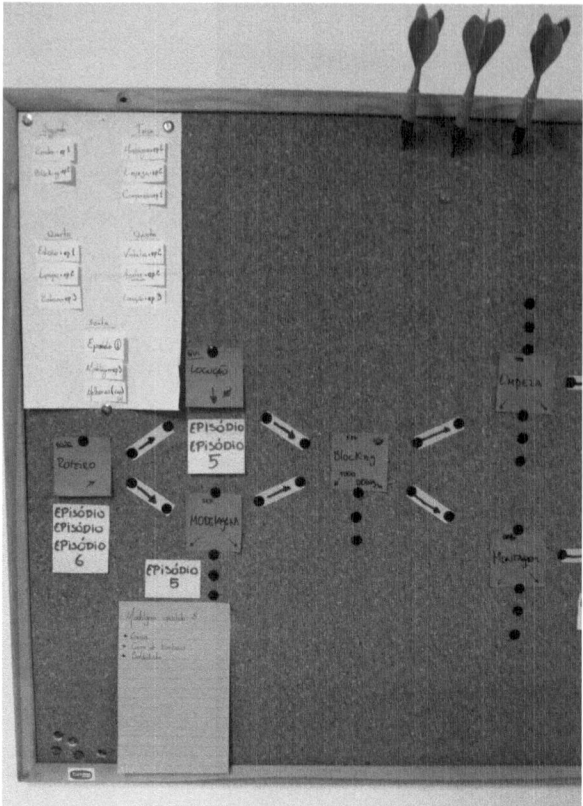

Fig. 3. Approximate view of the first part of the Kanban Board.

With this new format, another experimentation cycle was planned and exe-cuted, and the first three episodes were delivered. Once again, comparing the rel-evant points brought up during the CTA, the team displayed better engagement with self-management, dependence on the head animator was virtually nonexis-tent, the creation process became clear with the board illustrated in Fig. 2, and it was no longer subject to variability. The animations were delivered, although four days behind schedule.

4.4   Third Cycle: Lean Kanban

The last experiment cycle had the objective of eliminating delivery delays. To achieve that, we chose to explore Lean Kanban techniques [1] more deeply.

The team started to work on a continuous flow of episodes. Instead of doing Sprint Planning and defining what the next three episodes would cover, they decided that at each delivery they would present the episode to the PO and

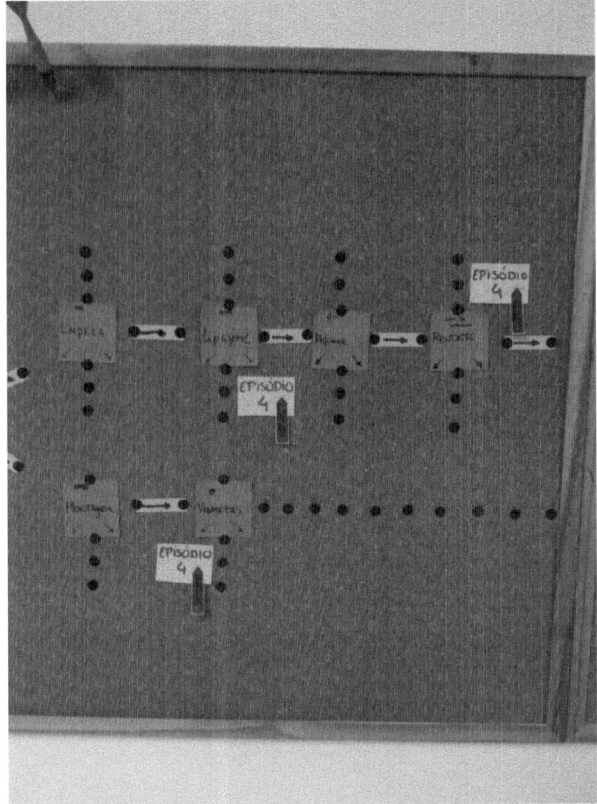

Fig. 4. Approximate view of the second part of the Kanban Board.

then define the following one to be created. The goal was to keep three episodes in production, thus generating a minimum reserve of episodes.

With the Work in Progress restriction, the team started to notice downtimes in the productive chain. Since the work they develop is highly specialized, they chose not to do swarming [1]. Instead, they decided to use the downtimes to automate animation items, thus reducing the effort needed to draw them and, consequently, the production time.

Automation is the creation of compositions that can be reused in different episodes in the series. For instance, the team had a few days off, so they used them to do Character Irrigation, which improves connecting joints such as arms, legs, neck and hands, making the motions more natural and without cuts. They also automated facial expressions and created some plugins to save time in future animations.

The team also agreed that each stage should last at most one work day. The script was written on a Wednesday, and from then each stage had to be

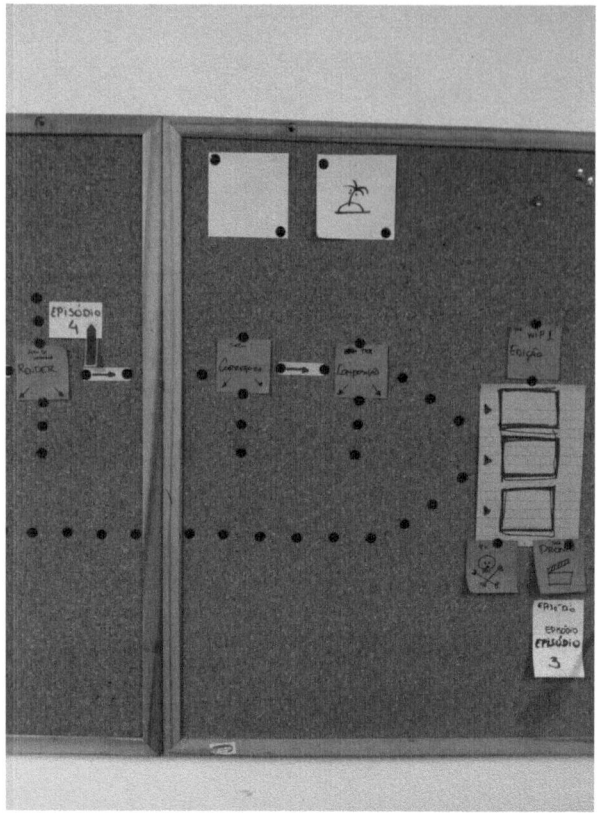

Fig. 5. Approximate view of the third part of the Kanban Board. (Color figure online)

executed in up to one business day. The only exception was Rendering, which was executed automatically and could take one weekend.

As an example of delay visualization, going back to Fig. 4 and assuming that it is Thursday on the first week, we could infer that Minute 1 of Episode 4 is one day ahead of schedule. Minute 2 of the same episode is one day behind schedule, because Refinement was supposed to take place on Thursday.

These changes allowed them to notice the delays and identify production bottlenecks. The episodes started to be delivered with a delay of two days.

5   Results

To collect the results obtained with the method described, at the end of the third Experiment Cycle a second interview was carried out with the animator in charge of the series [2]. The goal of this interview was to assess whether the proposed model was able to solve or mitigate the problems identified during the CTA (Fig. 1).

5.1   Management

Regarding the adoption of the method by the team, the interviewee said that there was some initial resistance. However, with time, the team started to feel represented on the board, which led them to start adopting self-management. The head animator no longer had to tell team members what to do, as they begun to select the tasks they had to work on. The daily meetings continued to happen, and the board was updated by the team.

The fact that the board represented the creation process saved significant time that was previously used for team management. There used to be a good deal of discussion about what each one should do. The head animator spent a lot of time organizing the process, but because he was also one of the animators, this caused delays in the animation development. After the process was detailed on the board, there was no more discussion. "I still act as responsible for the team, but now all I have to do is monitor", said the interviewee.

The board also brought two positive side effects. The first is that the area manager, who was not directly involved in the team's activities, realized the value of process transparency. "At a glance, he knows what is happening, if anything is delayed, what people are doing." [2] Another effect which emerged was the interest of other teams in using the model to start managing their creative processes.

5.2   Process

The board also resulted in a standardized creation process. Without variations in the stages, the team could now predict when an episode would be ready, when there was room for improvement and where there would be delays.

5.3   Deadlines

Regarding delay reduction, the interviewee said that the model adopted was crucial to identify delays and to find out which stages of the process had bottlenecks. Although the delays were reduced, they still happened during the experiment. However, assisted by the board, the animator responsible for the team was able to justify the need to hire one more employee for the team.

A few weeks after the interview, the head animator told us that a new member had joined the Creation Team and that the team started to deliver the episodes within one week. Figure 6 shows the reduction of the production time obtained in each experiment cycle.

5.4   Client

Finally, even with small delays in some episodes, the client's relationship with the producer became stable. The client is satisfied with the product being delivered.

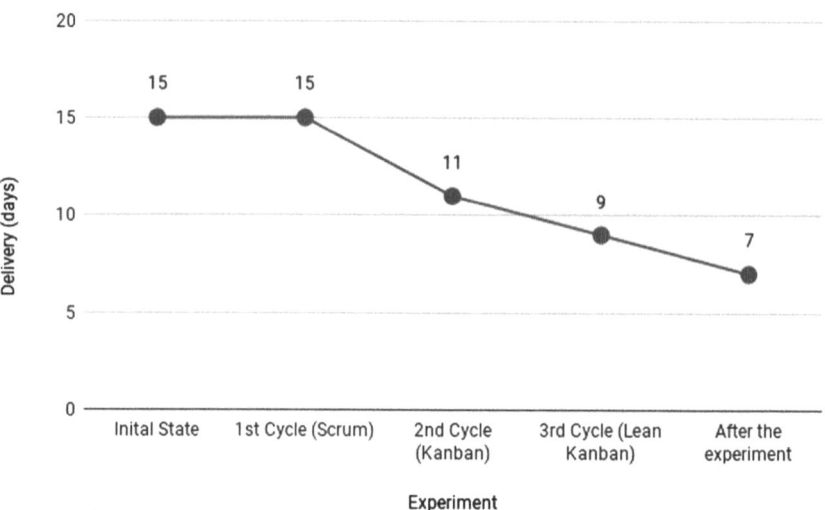

Fig. 6. Reduction of time of episode production per experiment cycle.

6   Conclusions and Future Work

The objective of this work was to build, collaboratively and iteratively, an Agile management model for the creation of 3D animations. We used Cognitive Task Analysis to understand the problem faced by the company and verify the results achieved when the model was implemented. As has been demonstrated, the action research method implemented through the experimentation cycle can assist in the continuous improvement of the solution proposed.

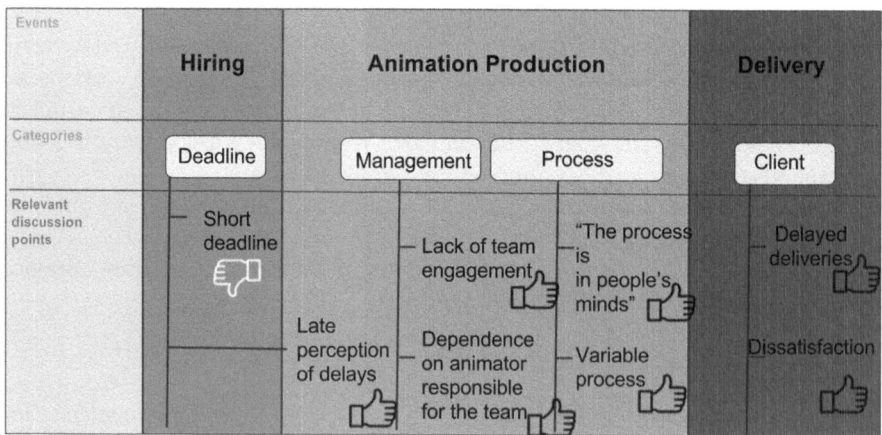

Fig. 7. Team response after the Agile adoption

Based on the perceived results, it is possible to claim that the method was able to solve problems related to the team's lack of engagement in managing the creation process, encouraged self-management, improved process visibility, reduced process variability, uncovered bottlenecks and reduced delays. Moreover, it was able to demonstrate the need to increase the number of professionals on the team so that the goals could be met in the turnaround time agreed upon with the client.

In the end, we sent the CTA analysis to the production team (Fig. 1). We asked them to indicate with a positive signal if they believed that the problem had been solved and with the negative signal if the problem had not been solved. The result is in Fig. 7. According to the them, with the exception of the Short deadline defined at the time of hiring, all major problems were solved.

In the future, this method will be applied to other teams in the same company to assess how it can be expanded to other contexts. The researchers are also searching for other video production companies to verify whether the method can be broadened and its results extrapolated beyond the company under study.

Acknowledgments. The authors of this work would like to thank Felipe Assis for his participation and great support of this work.

References

1. Anderson, D.: Kanban: Successful Evolutionary Change for Your Technology Business. Blue Hole Press, Seattle (2010)
2. Assis, F.: Final interview, July 2017. Gomes Filho, A.F.: Interviewer. São Paulo [s.n.] (2017)
3. Assis, F.: Initial interview, January 2017. Gomes Filho, A.F.: Interviewer. São Paulo [s.n.] (2017)
4. Boralli, A.B., França, R.B.: Applying continuous integration principles in safety-critical airborne software. In: Anais do 5° Workshop Brasileiro de Métodos Ágeis, pp. 1–12. INPE, São José dos Campos (2014)
5. Crandall, B., Klein, G.A., Hoffman, R.R.: Working Minds: A Practitioner's Guide to Cognitive Task Analysis. Mit Press, Cambridge (2006)
6. Gomes Filho, A.F., de Resende, C.F.C., de Toledo, R.: Usando métodos ágeis para ensinar métodos ágeis. In: Proceedings of the 5th Workshop Brasileiro de Métodos Ágeis, pp. 1–12. INPE, São José dos Campos (2014)
7. Gomes Filho, A.F., de Toledo, R.: Visual management and blind software developers. In: 2015 Agile Conference, pp. 31–39, August 2015
8. Lewin, K.: Action research and minority problems. J. Soc. Issues **2**(4), 34–46 (1946)
9. Lima, I.R., de Castro Freire, T., Costa, H.A.X.: Adapting and using scrum in a software research and development laboratory. Revista de Sistemas de Informação da FSMA **9**, 16–23 (2012)
10. Ries, E.: The Lean Startup: How Today's Entrepreneurs Use Continuous Innovation to Create Radically Successful Businesses. Crown Business, New York (2011)
11. Sutherland, J., Schwaber, K.: The scrum guide: The definitive guide to scrum: The rules of the game (2013). http://www.scrumguides.org/docs/scrumguide/v1/scrum-guide-us.pdf. Accessed 20 Dec 2015

12. Wingo, R.S., Tanik, M.M.: Using an agile software development methodology for a complex problem domain. In: SoutheastCon 2015, pp. 1–8, April 2015
13. Yothino, M., Rueangsirasak, W., Chaisricharoen, R.: Novel management model to increase visual effect productivity. In: 2013 13th International Symposium on Communications and Information Technologies (ISCIT), pp. 751–756, September 2013
14. Yothino, M., Rueangsirasak, W., Chaisricharoen, R.: Visual effects production improvement for thai film industry. In: The 4th Joint International Conference on Information and Communication Technology, Electronic and Electrical Engineering (JICTEE), pp. 1–7, March 2014

Concerns and Limitations in Agile Software Development: A Survey with Paraguayan Companies

Myrian R. Noguera Salinas[✉], Adolfo G. Serra Seca Neto[✉],
and Maria Claudia F. P. Emer[✉]

Academic Department of Informatics, Federal University of Technology,
Curitiba, Paraná, Brazil
michinoguera@gmail.com, adolfo@utfpr.edu.br,
mclaudia@dainf.ct.utfpr.edu.br

Abstract. The Agile Manifesto has been around form more than fifteen years and, all over the world, companies and researchers seek for understand their adoption stage, as well as the benefits, barriers, and limitations of agile methods. Although there are some survey studies at the global level, we know little about how the Paraguayan software community is adopting agile methods. The present work conducted a research to characterize the current stage of adoption, initial concerns and barriers on the implementation of agile methods in software development companies in Paraguay. An online survey was sent to managers of 53 Paraguayan companies. Of these, 9 (17%) managers responded. The main concern about adopting agile methods (44.44% of respondents) was the lack of reliability in product quality if developed using agile methods. The main barrier was the lack of experience (66.66%) of the companies.

Keywords: Agile methods · Agile Adoption · Survey
Software development enterprise

1 Introduction

Agile Software Development (ASD) was formally presented to the software engineering community in 2001 in a document called "Agile Manifesto", which mentions a set of core values and principles that emphasized Agility, in other words, the ability to adapt to fast volatile requirements [1]. However, agile principles don't suggest specific activities or artifacts; these are defined in a number of methods and practices such as Scrum, Extreme Programming (XP), Test Driven Development, Lean Software Development, Kanban etc. Practices vary and focus on different aspects of agile principles and address different problems in software development.

Since then, development with agile methods has attracted the attention of many researchers. Most of the available studies report experiences, generally positive, with their application in specific organizations and projects and, therefore, are hardly generalizable.

Motivated by the current popularity of agile methods and the interest of the first author (of Paraguayan nationality), we decided to investigate the concerns and

© Springer International Publishing AG 2018
V. A. Santos et al. (Eds.): WBMA 2017, CCIS 802, pp. 77–87, 2018.
https://doi.org/10.1007/978-3-319-73673-0_6

limitations to the adoption of agile methods. The remainder of this paper is organized as follows. Section 2 is the literature review followed by Sect. 3, which outlines objectives and research methodology. In Sect. 4, we analyse the results, and Sect. 5 presents the conclusion.

2   Literature Review

The term "Agile Methodologies" emerged in 2001, when a group of software development practitioners decided to meet in the US to discuss ways to improve the performance of their projects. They wrote a document entitled *The Agile Manifesto*. Methods and practices like TDD [21], Pair Programming [22] and Planning Poker [23], related to this manifesto, have been increasingly adopted in recent years.

Several authors have pointed out the advantages of agile methods, with their emphasis on individuals and iterative processes, client collaboration on formal contracts and negotiations, and responsiveness to rigid planning [8–12, 15–18]. However, there are few studies on adoption difficulties [8, 13, 14, 19, 20].

A survey conducted by VersionOne in 2016 suggested the main difficulties in adopting agile methods are: organizational culture in disagreement with agile values, (63%) and lack of skills or experience with agile methods (47%).

Another research [3, 13] was conducted in 2013 to characterize the current stage of adoption and adaptation of agile methods in Brazil. The results showed that the main concern in adopting the agile methods was the lack of documentation. In addition, the major barrier to broad adoption was the ability to change organizational culture.

In February 2015, both Gartner and Software Advice [4, 5] launched research and analysis on agile life-cycle management or project management tools. Of the project managers who responded, 49% say that coaching others is a common challenge they face, especially when adopting agile culture.

Another literature review study [6] focused on the current challenges of this agile movement. The most significant were team management, agility in distributed teams, prioritization of requirements, documentation, change requirement, organizational culture, process and monitoring, and feedback.

3   Objectives and Methodology

3.1   Definition of Goals

The main objective of our study was to characterize the current adoption stage, barriers and limitations regarding the use of agile methods in software development companies in Paraguay.

3.2   Methodology

For the accomplishment of the study a research was prepared by means of an online survey. The following are the steps performed in the study (Fig. 1):

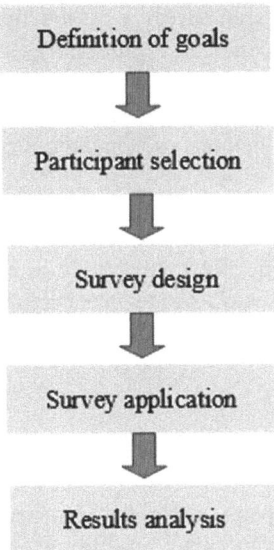

Fig. 1. Methodology adopted

Participant selection. A common problem when conducting an online survey is finding the right respondents and collecting enough answers so that you have relevant data. Our primary concern, therefore, was to find the right respondents, whose response is valuable enough to analyse the end result as managers and development managers. In our research, the questionnaire was disseminated directly to the directors or development managers of the companies.

According to the list provided by the Directorio de la Red de Inversiones y Exportaciones (REDIEX), which belongs to the Ministerio de Industria y Comercio de Paraguay, there are 53 companies registered in the Software Development category in Paraguay. The questionnaire was sent to all the companies on the list and 9 of them answered.

Survey design. We created an online questionnaire that consisted of ten multiple-choice questions.

The first section of this survey has general information. The details sought include the name of the organization to which the respondent belongs, the position, and how many people in total are employed in the company.

The second section deals with the adoption of agile methods, in which the questions were structured in such a way as to answer the main issues of adoption: concerns and barriers. The questions were, for instance, how many years of experience do you have using agile methods (to understand the extent of company familiarity with agile development) and what were the difficulties of adoption (to identify the reasons).

The last section complements previous data with the percentage of projects developed using agile methods.

Survey application. The research survey was directly disclosed to the directors or development managers of the companies through an e-mail, to which they responded by filling out the online questionnaire.

The participants were mainly representatives who had full knowledge of the company policies, the various methods used and the time the company has been using process development.

Result analysis. The analysis of the results was based on the answers that we received through the online questionnaire. Responses were carefully analysed in order to get accurate results based on the research. The main concern was to interpret the information in the wrong way, which would definitely not serve the purpose of our investigation.

4   Results

The data collected with the help of the form gave us a clear idea of the respondent and his position. Most of the participants are Project Managers or President of the Company, 33.33% in both cases, which ensures a responsible and official response (Fig. 2) and also confirms the current use of agile methods by 100% of the participants (Fig. 3).

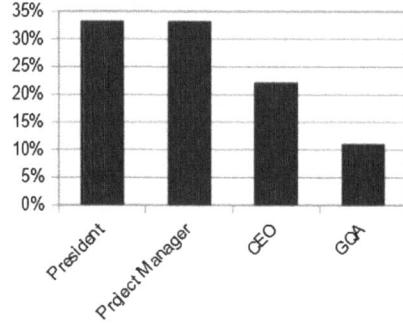   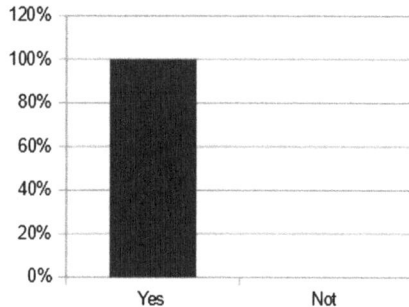

Fig. 2. Participant's role   **Fig. 3.** Does the company use agile methods?

Another important feature is the size of the software development team. Most (66.66%) of the companies have up to 20 employees in their team (Fig. 4).

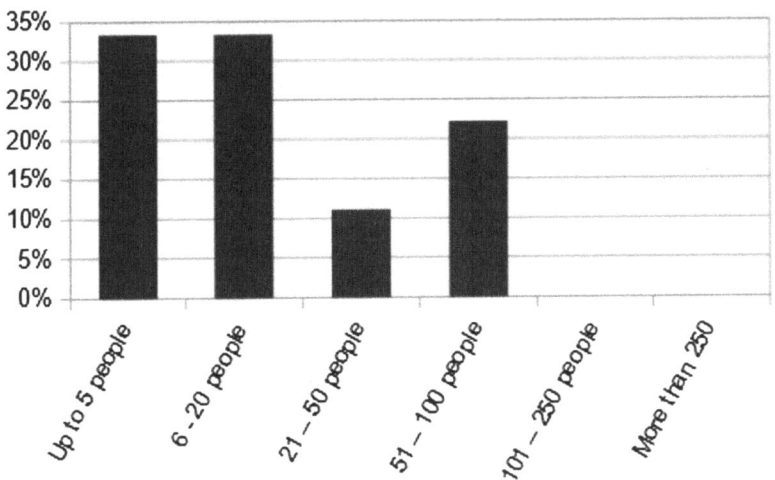

Fig. 4. Size of organization

One of the main themes of this research details the following concerns (Fig. 5):

- Inability to scale: Corresponds to the lack of organizational capacity to make the shift to agile methods.
- Reduced software quality: It's the perception of lack of reliability in delivering a quality product or ensuring customer satisfaction.
- Development team opposed to change: Occurs when developers are not convinced or motivated to make the move to agile methods.
- Lack of early planning: When participants are unaware of the activities needed to make the change because of lack of planning.
- Internal company regulations: When standards or company rules don't conform to the principles of the methods.
- No concerns: They had no concerns about adopting the methods.

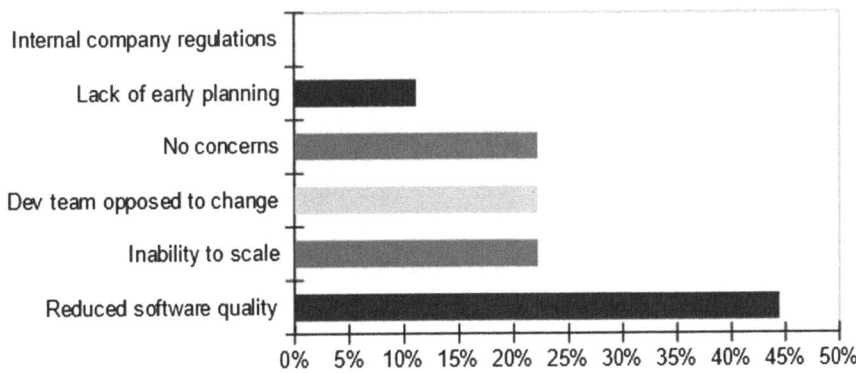

Fig. 5. Concerns about adopting agile

The data show that 44.44% of the participants had concerns about software quality when adopting agile methods. Other significant reasons are: inability to escalate, with 22.22%, and development team resistant to changes, with 22.22%.

Other important theme is identifying barriers to further adoption in the enterprise (Fig. 6). The reasons are detailed as follows:

- Company's internal rules or standards: When the company's rules don't match with the principles of agile methods.
- Budget constraints: The company has no budget for the broad adoption, but it has already implemented agile methods in some of its projects.
- Project complexity: The company also works with large and complex projects and uses agile methods to develop small projects.
- Customer collaboration: The client has no interest in participating in meetings and other activities appropriate to the agile methods or techniques used.
- Confidence in the ability to scale: Corresponds to difficulties to make the change to agile methods in order to increase its scale. That is, the difficulty in using agile methods in more projects and/or bigger projects.
- Lack of experience: The team does not have sufficient experience for the wide adoption of agile methods.
- Other: Other reasons not mentioned on the list.
- None: They had no barriers in adopting agile methods.

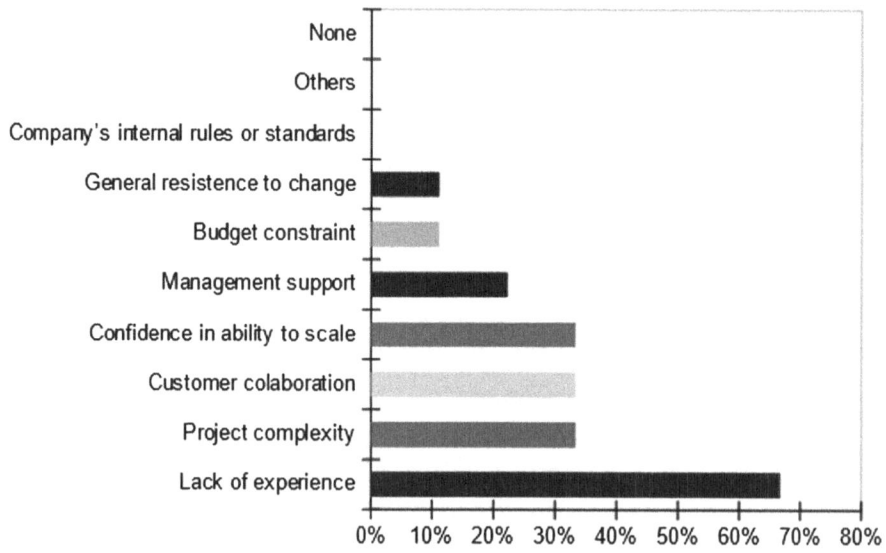

Fig. 6. Barriers to further Agile Adoption

The factors which are mainly chosen as main barriers to the adoption of agile methods (Fig. 6) are: (a) lack of experience with 66.66%, (b) project complexity, 33.33% (c) customer collaboration, with 33.33% and (d) confidence in the ability to scale with 33.33%.

Experience time is an important factor for the wide adoption of agile methods. The majority (55.56%) of the participating companies have average experience of 1 to 2 years (Fig. 7).

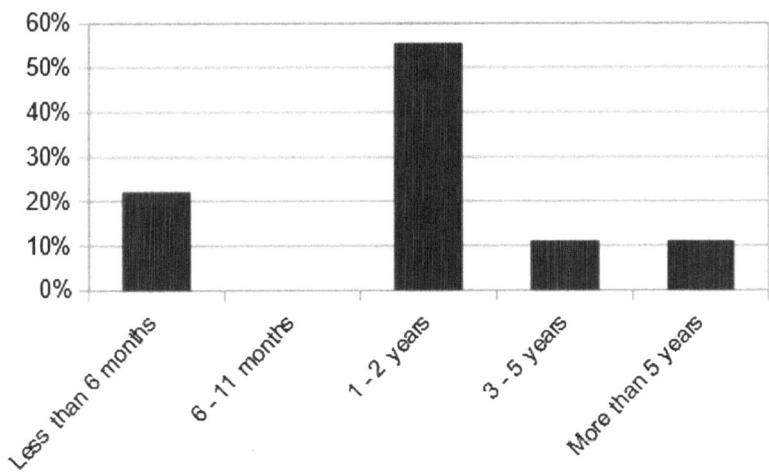

Fig. 7. Company experience with agile

The choices of methods and techniques are also fundamental according to the knowledge, the characteristics of the team and of the company (Figs. 8 and 9). Most of the companies interviewed prefer Scrum and the most used practices are: Unit tests with

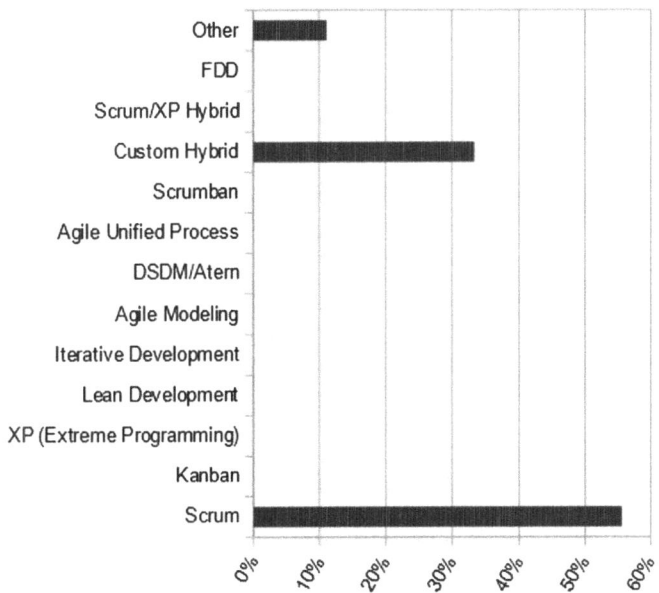

Fig. 8. Agile methodology used

55.56%, Short iterations with 44.44%, Backlogs prioritized with 33.33%, Daily meeting with 22, 22%, Retrospectives with 22,22%, Release planning with 22,22%, Continuous integration with 22,22% and Open work area with 22,22%.

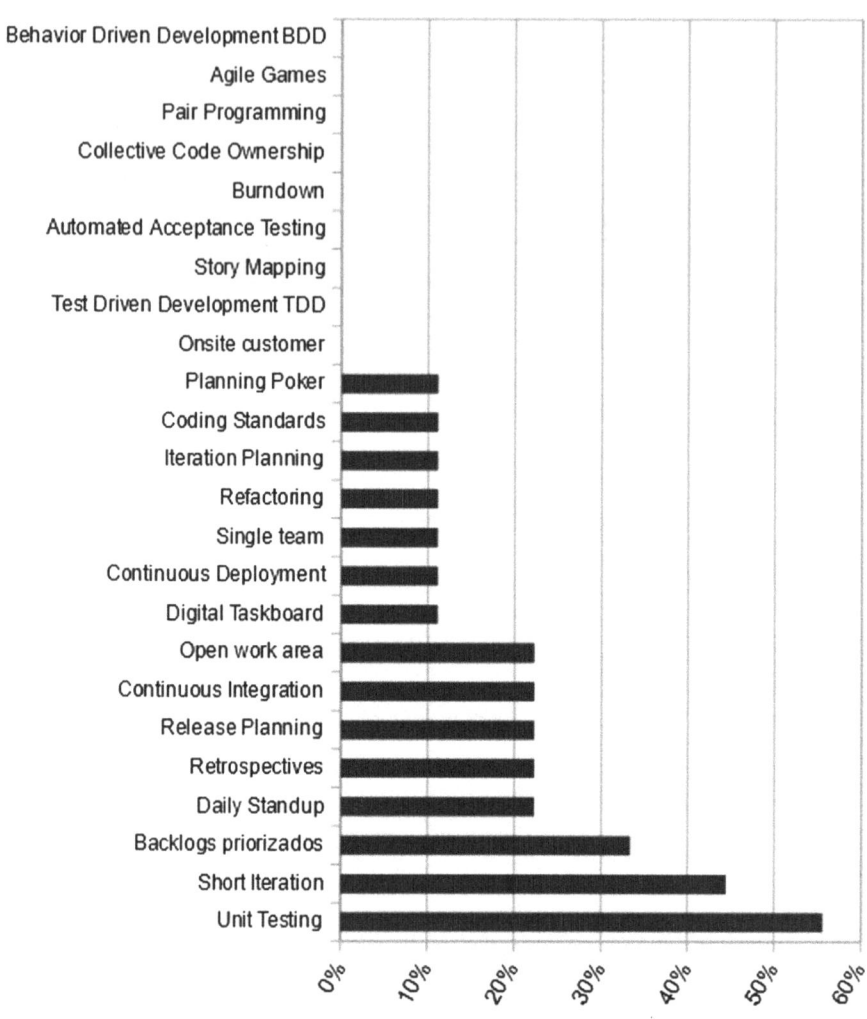

Fig. 9. Agile techniques used

Another data that allows us to visualize the adoption level is the quantity of projects developed with agile methods (Fig. 10). The majority (55.56%) of the companies used agile methods in 50% or more of their projects.

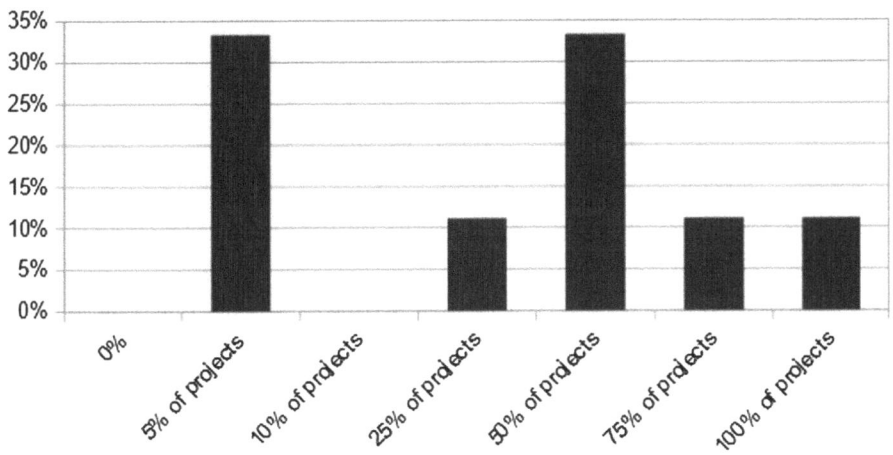

Fig. 10. Number of projects using agile methods

5 Discussion

When analyzing the results obtained, we can see that it was possible to identify similarities with the study conducted by VersionOne [2], mainly in the difficulties for the adoption of agile methods: organizational culture in disagreement with agile values (63%) and lack of skills or experience with agile methods (47%). Our study shows that the main barrier to the full adoption of agile methods in Paraguay is the lack of experience (66.66%). One of the possible causes may be the lack of training in agile methods and techniques, according to the opinions expressed by people related to the agile community in Paraguay.

In three aspects our results were very similar to those obtained in [13]: total size of the technology team, experience of the company in agile methods and most used method (Scrum). The main differences were related to:

- Percentage of projects carried out with agile methods. In [13], 30.4% of the companies developed all of their projects using agile methods. In our study, 11.11% of companies do the same;
- Profile of participants in the survey. In [13], 18.5% of respondents were developers. In our study, by the very design of the research, no developer was a respondent.

The greatest concern for the initial adoption reflects the following: 44.44% of participants had concerns about software quality at the time they adopted agile methods. The other reasons are: inability to scale, 22.22%, and development team resistant to changes, 22.22%. We believe that the concern with lack of reliability in software quality is probably the result of lack of knowledge or training on agile methods and techniques. Agile methods propose a better response to client expectations, so that more software quality is what should be expected.

It is important to note that the results cannot be generalized statistically because it corresponds to a preliminary study that aims to be complemented with more data to be significant and to allow a more concrete visualization of the mentioned scenario.

6 Conclusions

This research was carried out with the purpose of identifying the level of adoption of agile methods in software development companies in Paraguay, raising the barriers and the concerns for their implementation. The answers to the questionnaire reveal that these companies experience the use of methods and techniques, and the main concerns they reported are (a) reduced software quality, (b) change resistant development team, and (c) inability to scale.

The barriers reported are (a) little experience, (b) confidence in the ability to scale agile methods, (c) little or no customer collaboration, and (d) complexity or size of projects. Another interesting result is that more than 50% of the companies adopt the Scrum Framework.

References

1. Beck, K., Beedle, M., Van Bennekum, A., Cockburn, A., Cunninngham, W., Fowler, M., Grenning, J., Highsmith, J., Hunt, A., Jeffries, R., Kern, J., Marick, B., Martin, R., Mellor, S., Schwaber, K., Sutherland, J., Thomas, D.: Manifiesto for agile software development (2001). http://agilemanifesto.org/
2. VersionOne Inc.: 11th Annual State of Agile Survey (2016). http://www.versionone.com/
3. Melo, C., Santos, V., Corbucci, H., Katayama, E., Goldman, A., Kon, F.: Métodos ágeis no Brasil: estado da prática em times e organizações, Relatório Técnico RT-MAC-2012-03. Departamento de Ciência da Computação. IME-USP (2012)
4. InfoQ: Gartner and Software Advice examine Agile Lifecycle Management Tools (2015). https://www.infoq.com/news/2015/02/agile-management-tools
5. SoftwareAdvise: Agile Project Management Software User Report – 2015 (2015). http://www.softwareadvice.com/resources/agile-project-management-user-trends-2015/
6. Resti, W., Rahayu, P., Indra, D.: Challenges in agile software development: a systematic literature review. In: 2016 International Conference on Computer Science and Information Systems (ICACSIS), Malang, Indonesia, pp. 155–164. IEEE Xplore (2016). https://doi.org/10.1109/ICACSIS.2016.7872736
7. Kamei, F., Pinto, G., Cartaxo, B., Vasconcelos, A.: On the benefits/limitations of agile software development: an interview study with Brazilian companies. In: 21st Evaluation and Assessment in Software Engineering Conference (EASE), Karlskrona, Sweden, pp. 154–159. ACM Digital Library (2017). https://doi.org/10.1145/3084226.3084278
8. Nazir, N., Hasteer, N., Bansal, A.: A survey on agile practices in the Indian IT industry. In: 6th International Conference Cloud System and Big Data Engineering (Confluence), India. IEEEXplore (2016). https://doi.org/10.1109/CONFLUENCE.2016.7508196
9. Hoda, R., Salleh, N., Grundy, J., Mien Tee, H.: Systematic literature reviews in agile software development: a tertiary study. Inf. Softw. Technol. **85**, 60–70 (2017). https://doi.org/10.1016/j.infsof.2017.01.007. ScienceDirect

10. Pinto, J., Serrador, P.: Does agile work? A quantitative analysis of agile project success. Int. J. Project Manage. **33**, 1040–1051 (2015). https://doi.org/10.1016/j.ijproman.2015.01.006. ScienceDirect

11. Dyba, T., Dingsøyr, T.: Empirical studies of agile software development: a systematic review. Inf. Softw. Technol. **50**, 833–859 (2008). https://doi.org/10.1016/j.infsof.2008.01.006. ScienceDirect

12. Chow, T., Cao, D.: A survey study of critical success factors in agile software projects. J. Syst. Softw. **81**, 961–971 (2008). https://doi.org/10.1016/j.jss.2007.08.020. ScienceDirect

13. Melo, C., Santos, V., Katayama, E., Corbucci, H., Prikladnicki, R., Goldman, A., Kon, F.: The evolution of agile software development in Brazil – Education, research and the state of the practice. J. Braz. Comput. Soc. 523–552 (2013). https://doi.org/10.1007/s13173-013-0114-x. Springer Link

14. Solinski, A., Petersen, K.: Prioritizing agile benefits and limitations in relation to practice usage. Softw. Qual. J. **24**, 447–482 (2016). https://doi.org/10.1007/s11219-014-9253-3. Springer Link

15. Petersen, K., Wohlin, C.: A comparison of issues and advantages in agile and incremental development between state of the art and an industrial case. J. Syst. Softw. **82**, 1479–1490 (2009). https://doi.org/10.1016/j.jss.2009.03.036. ScienceDirect

16. Pikkarainen, M., Haikara, J., Salo, O., Abrahamsson, P., Still, J.: The impact of agile practices on communication in software development. Empir. Softw. Eng. **13**, 303–337 (2008). https://doi.org/10.1007/s10664-008-9065-9. Springer Link

17. Chandra, S., Kumar, V., Kumar, U.: Identifying some important success factors in adopting agile software development practices. J. Syst. Softw. **82**, 1869–1890 (2009). https://doi.org/10.1016/j.jss.2009.05.052. ScienceDirect

18. Laanti, M., Salo, O., Abrahamsson, P.: Agile methods rapidly replacing traditional methods at Nokia: a survey of opinions on agile transformation. Inf. Softw. Technol. **53**, 276–290 (2011). https://doi.org/10.1016/j.infsof.2010.11.010. ScienceDirect

19. Javdani, T., Ziaei, M.: Agile transition and adoption human-related challenges and issues: a Grounded Theory approach. Comput. Hum. Behav. **62**, 257–266 (2016). https://doi.org/10.1016/j.chb.2016.04.009. ScienceDirect

20. Corbucci, H., Melo, C., Santos, V., Katayama, E., Goldman, A., Kon, F.: Genesis and evolution of the agile movement in Brazil - a perspective from the academia and the industry. In: 25th Brazilian Symposium on Software Engineering (SBES). IEEE Xplore (2011). https://doi.org/10.1109/SBES.2011.26

21. Bissi, W., Neto, A., Emer, M.C.: The effects of test driven development on internal quality, external quality and productivity: a systematic review. Inf. Softw. Technol. **74**, 45–54 (2016). https://doi.org/10.1016/j.infsof.2016.02.004. Science Direct

22. Lima, V., Neto, A., Emer, M.C.: Investigação experimental e práticas ágeis: ameaças à validade de experimentos envolvendo a prática ágil Programação em par. In: Proceedings of the 3rd Brazilian Workshop on Agile Methods (WBMA'2012) (2012). https://doi.org/10.5329/RESI.2014.1301005

23. Tissot, A., Neto, A., Emer, M.C.: Influence of the review of executed activities utilizing Planning Poker. In: 29th Brazilian Symposium on Software Engineering (SBES). IEEE Xplore (2015). https://doi.org/10.1109/SBES.2015.26

Scrum and the 10 Personal Entrepreneurial Competencies of Empretec

Ludimila Monjardim Casagrande[✉]

Apoema Consultoria, Vitória, ES, Brazil
ludimila.casagrande@apoemaconsultoria.com.br

Abstract. This article presents the correlations between the practices applied by the Scrum framework and the 10 Personal Entrepreneurial Competencies (PECs) associated with the performance of successful entrepreneurs and validated by the United Nations Conference on Trade and Development (UNCTAD). This is based on our observation as consultants and on the experience in implementing the Scrum framework in software companies over the last 5 years.

Keywords: Scrum · Empretec · Entrepreneurial profile
Personal Entrepreneurial Competencies · Project management
Software engineering

1 Introduction

For businessmen the ideal company is composed by employees that think and act as entrepreneurs, that is, by persistent and committed people, focused on results, well defined goals and on client satisfaction. Thus, aiming to disseminate the use of Scrum as a management model in software development companies, and suggesting a way to develop such desired skills, this article presents the correlation between the Personal Entrepreneurial Competencies (PECs), associated with the performance of successful entrepreneurs, and the practices supported and implemented by Scrum. This correlation is based on our experience, observation and perception as consultants and trainers in the software industry.

2 Empretec Personal Entrepreneurial Competencies

The Personal Entrepreneurial Competencies (PECs) referenced in this article have been identified and scientifically proven by research initially carried out in the United States. Currently, PECs are disseminated by Empretec, an entrepreneurial education program designed by the United Nations (UN), promoted in about 34 countries and implemented in Brazil through SEBRAE (Brazilian Service for Support to Micro and Small Enterprises). Empretec was created more than 20 years ago and is one of the greatest achievements in the history of SEBRAE. The program also develops behavioral changes, promotes the revision of concepts and attitudes and prepares the entrepreneur for the market and for life [1].

© Springer International Publishing AG 2018
V. A. Santos et al. (Eds.): WBMA 2017, CCIS 802, pp. 88–94, 2018.
https://doi.org/10.1007/978-3-319-73673-0_7

The PECs developed in Empretec are listed in Table 1.

Table 1. Empretec Personal Entrepreneurial Competencies (PECs) [2].

Empretec Personal Entrepreneurial Competencies (PECs)	
1. Systematic Planning and Monitoring	6. Fulfilling Commitments
2. Goal Setting	7. Demand for Efficiency and Quality
3. Opportunity-seeking and Initiative	8. Information-seeking
4. Taking Calculated Risks	9. Persuasion and Networking
5. Persistence	10. Independence and Self-confidence

3   Correlations with Scrum

3.1   Systematic Planning and Monitoring

Successful entrepreneurs plan by dividing large activities into tasks with defined deadlines and they constantly revise their plans taking into account the obtained results and circumstantial changes.

Scrum does precisely the same because it follows an incremental and iterative development approach, in which the project scope is subdivided and worked into parts. These parts or functional blocks are implemented in development cycles called Sprints, which have a maximum duration of one month. At each Sprint start, a planning meeting is held in which the development team establishes the Sprint goals with the client. These goals state what can be completed and delivered to the client during the Sprint period.

During the subsequent days, the team meets daily to assess their progress, identify problems and possible impediments, and carry out or plan corrective actions, if needed. This way, the team stays in sync and maintains their work under control.

At the end of each Sprint, the team presents the achieved results to the client at a review meeting and, if the goals have not been fully met, states what has not been accomplished and presents their reasons. At this meeting, the client can inspect, give feedback on the work done and correct any deviations caused by communication problems.

Shortly after the review, a retrospective meeting takes place in which the Scrum team self-assesses, identifies relevant issues and problems, discusses what people have done well and what they could have done better, and lastly defines a plan of action to prevent certain problems from recurring and to mitigate risks in general.

These planning and monitoring events are systematically repeated in each development cycle, promoting a continuous process of inspection and adaptation.

3.2   Goal Setting

As previously mentioned, in Scrum the Sprint goals are set at the planning meeting held on the first day of each new cycle. What stands out here is that these goals are set based on the size, experience, and estimates made by the team members themselves. Therefore, in Scrum, the estimates are not defined by the business department or by top management people. Respecting the deadlines defined by the team is essential to attain the team's commitment to the established goals. In addition, the team can have direct contact with the client to clarify their questions so that they can better estimate and plan the commitments made at the Sprint. Since a Sprint lasts a maximum of one month, the goals are always short-term and are evaluated at the end of this period.

3.3   Opportunity-Seeking and Initiative

The pursuit of opportunities is inherent in the development of software projects, without which the projects simply do not exist, but what we want to highlight here is the individual pursuit of opportunities and initiatives of the development team members. Scrum promotes the development of this competency by adopting a management model in which teams are self-organized and in which the members themselves take the initiative to perform certain project activities. This means that in Scrum the activities are not assigned or imposed on each developer by a project manager, the developer himself requests or volunteers to perform an activity. Alternatively, the team, in consensus, indicates the one they consider the best member to perform each task, thus valuing the outstanding abilities of each one, enhancing the team's skills and better tapping the resources.

Consequently, people feel more valued for having their specific skills recognized by the team and feel motivated to have the opportunity to work on what they like best or have the chance to take up a challenge and learn how to execute a different task.

3.4   Taking Calculated Risks

Taking calculated risks means putting oneself in situations that involve challenges or moderate risks and that is exactly what Scrum does. Because it is a highly flexible model, Scrum accepts the changes and is prepared to deal with them. Scrum understands that changes in requirements and unexpected circumstances are inherent in the extremely volatile and dynamic nature of software projects. Scrum can deal well with changes by following the incremental and iterative approach and because it works with open scope; this means that in Scrum projects it is not necessary to define or know the full scope at the beginning of the project. The requirements that make up the scope are gradually identified and defined, allowing clients to mature the project goals throughout the development process. The iterative approach, with short cycles, also allows for greater involvement and frequent client feedback, which allows deviations from the desired outcome to be identified more quickly, reducing the risk of propagating a mistake or misunderstanding, within the one-month deadline.

In addition, to take calculated risks, one must control them, evaluate alternatives, and act to minimize them, since, despite the scope flexibility, many clients naturally impose cost and time constraints. How does Scrum control this? Given the limitations of the project, each Sprint requirements are prioritized by the client, who should request that the most important and highest business value requirements are carried out first, obviously respecting any technical constraints. By adopting this approach, the fulfillment of what is really essential is guaranteed in the initial stages of the project. From there, the client continues to prioritize what shall be developed, bearing in mind that eventually some requirements, considered less important, will need to be discarded. The assignment of the degree of relevance of a requirement, in this way, must always be carried out by the client so that he assumes responsibility for the obtained results and especially for the eliminated items, thus maximizing the chances of success of the project since ultimately, success means client satisfaction and earned value.

The other way to control risks is through inspection and adaptation, two of the three pillars of Scrum. Per Schwaber and Sutherland, authors of the official Scrum Guide, "each event in Scrum is a formal opportunity to inspect and adapt something" [3]. To minimize the risk of not meeting client expectations in terms of team productivity, once the scope is open, Sprint goals are collaboratively established in Sprint Planning, thereby setting expectations and goals to be achieved and allowing them to be monitored.

The most important Scrum events in terms of control are the Sprint end events, that is, Sprint Review and Sprint Retrospective. Scrum considers that having the team members present the Sprint results directly to the client increases the degree of responsibility and commitment of the group, since it enables people to be valued when there is merit and creates discomfiture when there is no commitment to undertaken goals.

In addition, the review meeting promotes alignment between provider and client and allows the client to inspect, evaluate, give feedback, acquire knowledge and adapt the developing work, increasing their chances of achieving their goals.

In the retrospective meeting, the Scrum team inspects how the last Sprint went with regards to people, relationships, practices, and tools; it identifies and sorts the key items that went well and the potential improvements; and it creates an action plan to implement the identified issues and to mitigate risks in general, thus closing a cycle of inspection and adaptation and promoting continuous improvement.

3.5 Demand for Efficiency and Quality

In addition to the previously mentioned permanent work of inspection and adaptation of the processes and people, continuous attention to technical excellence and good design is one of the agile software principles [4], and since Scrum is currently the most widely used agile "method" [4], this base principle could not be ignored. Since Scrum is not a prescriptive model, it admits that many techniques and good software development practices are associated with its framework. Therefore, Scrum projects often use the implementation of automated tests, the adoption of TDD (Test Driven Development), continuous integration, pair programming, peer review, refactoring, among many other practices and techniques that promote software quality and efficiency.

3.6 Fulfilling Commitments

Commitment is simply one of the five Scrum values, as can be seen in Fig. 1 of Scrum.org [6]. In Scrum, people personally commit to achieving the goals of the entire team. Commitment includes collaborating with your work partners or taking responsibility in their place, if needed, to finalize a task and to achieve a particular goal. Commitment also involves staying focused on the client, striving to understand the real needs of their business and contributing to the fact that the developed software product, in fact, adds value, thus achieving customer satisfaction and loyalty.

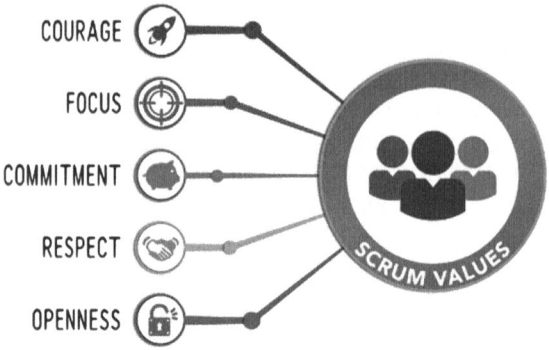

Fig. 1. Scrum values by Scrum.org.

Scrum encourages commitment by supporting team self-organization, setting clear goals in planning meetings, allowing developers to be able to take on certain responsibilities and tasks, removing the traditional role of the project manager, sharing the project responsibility, stimulating real teamwork by explicitly establishing that everyone is responsible for all the tasks and goals set for the project and that, when the goals set in a Sprint are not met, it means that everyone has failed.

3.7   Information-Seeking

The transparency factor and non-hierarchical structure of Scrum teams allow any member of the development team to interact directly with the client or third parties to seek relevant and assertive information for the execution of their activities in the project, thus providing opportunities for people to develop their communication skills. It is worth emphasizing that communication problems are often pointed out as one of the main factors responsible for the failure of software projects. Moreover, a self-organized team demands dialogue and joint decision-making, which favors interpersonal relationships and makes the communication channels between the less and more experienced members of the project more open. Finally, software development alone requires investigations, research and expert consultations in order to solve particular problems or to obtain technical assistance, as the technologies evolve very rapidly.

3.8   Persistence

The characteristic persistence is closely linked to courage, which is one of the Scrum values. For Scrum, the team has the courage to do the right thing and work through problems. It is often impossible to meet client needs by attempting to implement a closed scope or by following a strictly defined plan at the beginning of the project - as the traditional development approach suggests. Over time "meeting the scope" becomes incompatible with "doing what needs to be done to add value to the client's business". It is in this respect that a client who requires a closed scope, with the intention of conducting a safer negotiation with the supplier, betrays himself; because real projects mature, evolve and change over time, demanding flexibility and frequent changes. Therefore, the team must always be prepared to accommodate contingencies and changes, and to constantly adapt to a new scenario. Certainly, being flexible is much more difficult and complex than following a well-defined plan, which requires team persistence and an extraordinary effort to achieve their goals.

3.9 Persuasion and Networking

Because the Scrum Team is self-organized and does not have a hierarchical structure, technical project decisions are always made together. This makes possible solutions and consequent decisions to be broadly discussed, forcing team members to develop their ability to argue for or against a given solution, and therefore to promote persuasion skills in team members. This also favors the emergence of natural leaders in the project, based on respect and recognition. In addition, because the responsibility for the project success is shared, everyone needs to act in search of solutions and consequently, they often need to turn to third parties. In this way, team members use key people to solve problems, thus strengthening relationships with external people and their networks.

3.10 Independence and Self-confidence

Once again, the adoption of a self-organizing and non-hierarchical team allows team members to have greater independence and autonomy. The Scrum team members define the activity estimates and decide the goals of each Sprint together with the client, thus increasing their degree of involvement, responsibility, and commitment to these goals. Shared responsibility and joint decisions value the individuals and the contributions of each one, thus increasing their self-confidence.

In addition, the constant adaptation needs of the development model proposed by Scrum requires the team to have more maturity, security, and control to deal with adverse situations and keep going forward in search of success.

4 Conclusion

We can conclude that the framework proposed by Scrum is fully adherent and helps to develop in people the Personal Entrepreneurial Competencies contained in the Empretec program of the United Nations. For these and other reasons, companies should at least consider the benefits they could have by abandoning the traditional command-and-control management model and by offering more autonomy to their team members so that they are able to exploit their best skills and potential - which will certainly translate into increased speed, productivity gains and financial return for the company.

The model proposed by Scrum increases the interaction and the degree of involvement of both the clients and the developers, also increasing their level of commitment to the goals to be achieved. In this way, Scrum promotes healthier relationships between companies and suppliers and more sustainable businesses, thus increasing the chances of success of both.

References

1. SEBRAE: Empretec - Manual do Participante, Brasília, DF (2011)
2. UNCTAD. Entrepreneurship Policy Framework and Implementation Guidance (2012)
3. Schwaber, K., Sutherland, J.: The scrum guide - the definitive guide to scrum: the rules of the game (2016)
4. Beck, K., Schwaber, K., Sutherland, J., et al.: Principles Behind the Agile Manifesto (2001). http://agilemanifesto.org/principles.html. Accessed 26 Oct 2017
5. Scrum Alliance. The 2016 State of Scrum Report (2016)
6. Scrum.org. The Home of Scrum: What is Scrum? https://www.scrum.org/resources/what-is-scrum. Accessed 26 Oct 2017

An Agile Approach Applied in Enterprise Project Management Office

Luis Gustavo Araujo Ferreira[1(✉)], Priscila Bibiana Viegas[1(✉)],
and Dagoberto Trento[2(✉)]

[1] University of Vale do Rio dos Sinos (UNISINOS), São Leopoldo, Brazil
`luis.gustavo.af@gmail.com`, `pribibiana@gmail.com`
[2] Federal University of Rio Grande do Sul (UFRGS), Porto Alegre, Brazil
`trentodagoberto@gmail.com`

Abstract. In a highly connected world, surrounded by many changes, companies need to adapt to remain competitive in the market. Many of the initiatives occur through projects, that need to be dynamic to meet the business need combined with the organization's strategic planning. The Project Management Office (PMO) in this scenario has the role of supporting the organization with tools and techniques to overcome this changes and ensure alignment with the organization's strategic initiatives. This paper presents an acting model for an Agile PMO putting the PMO at the center of the organizational changes being it the catalyst of information and the disseminator of good practices and knowledge to sustain the changes.

Keywords: Agile PMO · Agile project management
Exponential Organizations

1 Introduction

Companies are currently undergoing several transformations. The ever-changing market acts as a driver for companies to adapt to new scenarios. Most of the organizational transformations occur in companies through projects [1]. These projects need to be aligned with the organization's need through its strategic planning. In this sense, the role of the Project Management Office (PMO) is to help organizations plan, implement and monitor these projects so that they achieve their goals.

A great motivator of change in organizations is the digital transformation [2], where companies need to adapt technology to remain competitive in the market. Many organizations that not technologically evolve in the coming years will probably have difficulties in surviving in a competitive market. The companies that are currently guiding the market are those that have an exponential growth, called exponential organizations (ExO). They are organizations that grow rapidly, reach growth 10 times their size in just 2 to 3 years [3]. How to be prepared for the changes you have seen with this growth? What is the role of the PMO in this scenario?

The PMO must be prepared to adapt to these changes and often be the area where the company's strategic shall be supported to be supported to maintain communication

© Springer International Publishing AG 2018
V. A. Santos et al. (Eds.): WBMA 2017, CCIS 802, pp. 95–102, 2018.
https://doi.org/10.1007/978-3-319-73673-0_8

and engagement of senior management with the progress of the projects. According to the Project Management Institute (PMI), the focus of senior management organizations remains largely focused on the bridge between strategy formulation and execution. Thus, giving greater emphasis to be more agile, customer-focused and competitive [4].

The PMO, being an important agent in this entire process of transformation, must have mastery of models and techniques capable of supplying the organization. His own actions have to follow a model that allows it to adapt and change their focus to monitor the company's needs. The vision of where the PMO wants to reach, its goals, its objectives and its systematic monitoring of their actions becomes a focal point for the continuous delivery of PMO value to the organization.

In this context, this paper presents a role model for Agile PMO containing elements that support its operations amid a backdrop of many changes. This model can be applied in many organizations, especially in cases where there are many transformations.

2   Theoretical Foundation

2.1   Massive Transformative Purpose

In 2015 Salim Ismail proposed in his book [3] a concept called MTP, Massive Transformative Purpose. This is a concept that indicates what the company intends to do and not what it does. Its main purpose is to provide organizations with a purpose with a focus and goals that are transformative.

The MTP is a feature of the companies called Exponential Organization (ExO), whose impact (or result) is disproportionately large - at least ten times higher - compared to its peers, due to the use of new organizational techniques that leverage accelerated technologies [3].

These companies are guided through their MTP and present 10 attributes in common. Of these, 5 attributes are internal (SCALE) and are responsible for the creativity, growth and uncertainty of the business: Team on demand, Communities and Crowd, Algorithms, Leveraged Assets and Engagement. The other 5 attributes are external (IDEAS) and are responsible for order, control and stability: Interface, Dashboards, Experimentation, Autonomy and Social.

2.2   Objectives and Results

Many companies guide their management by setting objectives and results. In 1999 John Doerr introduced a new model for Google, which he had first learned in Intel, the Objective and Key Results (OKR), a framework for goal setting [5].

The OKR consists of clear definition of objectives and their results, being measurable, enabling them to be monitored and controlled. The OKR model is a standard for aligning company strategy with individual team goals [6]. An OKR should be described simply and clearly. The model suggests that it is written as follows: "I will (goal) measured by (the result set)." The OKR definition consists of two levels. A strategic level set by the organization with a one year horizon. The other level is the OKR defined by the team and has a horizon of three months.

2.3   Scrum Framework

Scrum is a framework created in the 90s, initially used for development and support of complex products. The framework has several good practices that can be adopted by different teams. Being a framework, it can be used as needed by the team. [7] The framework is used, partially or totally, by about 95% of organizations that use agile methods in their companies [8].

The Scrum framework is based on an empirical process based on three pillars: transparency, inspection and adaptation. Scrum consists of the Scrum team and their roles, events, artifacts and associated rules. Scrum rules link events, roles, and artifacts, managing relationships and interacting with each other. The Scrum team consists of three roles:

- Product Owner (PO): responsible for maximizing the value of the product to be delivered through the work that the development team will build;
- Scrum Master (SM): responsible for ensuring that the Scrum framework is understood by everyone on the team and that it is being followed;
- Developer: are responsible for making deliveries. They are organized and empowered by the organization to manage their work.

The events in the Scrum framework aim to create rhythms in deliveries and minimize the need to hold meetings not defined in Scrum. All events have a set time for their realization (time-box).

- Sprint: is the main Scrum event, its time-box is one month or less. This is the period of making deliveries;
- Sprint Planning: Sprint initial event, where your planning is done. The expected result for this ceremony is the definition of what will be done, how it will be done and the purpose of Sprint;
- Daily Scrum: daily meeting with 15 min time-box. In this meeting, each of the team must answer three questions: (1) what I did yesterday, (2) what I'll do today and (3) if there is any impediment to the performance of my activities;
- Sprint Review: is the time where the team presents Sprint deliveries and collects feedback, incrementing the backlog, if necessary. His time-box is 4 h for a one month Sprint;
- Sprint Retrospective: this ceremony is the opportunity the team has, to inspect at Sprint and create a plan to implement improvements in the next Sprint.

The artifacts are used to promote transparency and create opportunities for inspection and adaptation. The main artifacts are the Product Backlog, an ordered list of the actions/tasks the product needs, and the Sprint Backlog, a list of items that will be worked on in the following Sprint.

3   Methodology

The objective of this paper is to provide a model to enable the PMO to be the support for the organization in massive transformations (MTP), being guided by focus on deliverables and measurable results (OKR), through its team, joining efforts to realize the deliverables in periods of time (Agile). The Fig. 1 presents the performance model for an Agile PMO containing the elements necessary for its operation.

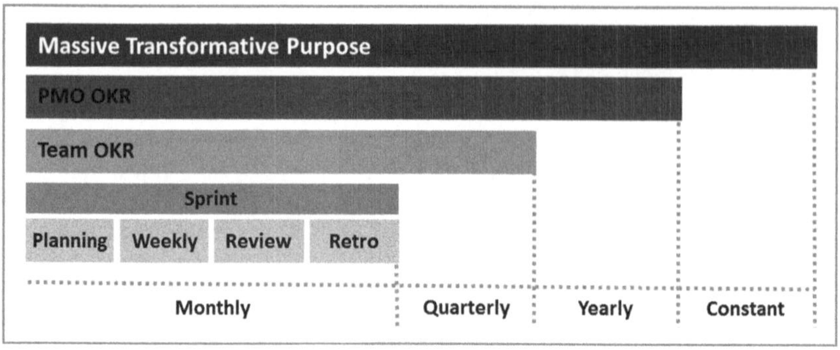

Fig. 1. Operating model of a PMO Agile. (Source: own authorship).

3.1 Agile PMO MTP

The massive transformative purpose is something that must be the great motivator of the PMO's existence. As Salim Ismail quotes in his book [3], an MTP needs to impact many people to be relevant and make sense.

This definition associated to a PMO means that his actions and initiatives need to transpire beyond the organization department and permeate throughout the organization. It is necessary to think about how their actions can positively impact everyone in your company.

Some PMOs are already considered Enterprise PMO [9] and their actions must act throughout the organization. In this case, the definition of the MTP is something easier to define because its vision of every organization is implicit in its purpose. Another type of PMO, considered departmental, needs a little more understanding about its scope of action to define its MTP. It is worth mentioning that the tendency is for the PMO to become more and more corporate, helping the organization to monitor strategic initiatives [4].

For the formulation of MTP it is necessary to seek together the senior management directing the PMO to organization. With this information, bring together the PMO team, search for the essence words to describe their purpose and formulate the main phrase of the MTP. Other information may be described in addition to the main sentence.

3.2 PMO OKR

The OKR PMO are the objectives and results that the area intends to achieve. These are OKR that will give direction to all other actions that the team will propose. They need to be in sync with the organization MTP definition.

The definition of these OKR occurs by the high management of the organization giving the direction of the PMO. The vision is one year and aims to answer the question, where the PMO wants to be a year from now.

The main purpose of this OKR is to challenge the team to make deliveries above expectations. These are goals that take the team from the comfort zone and make people rethink the way they work to achieve maximum performance. For this reason, these goals are rarely achieved and serve to constantly challenge the team.

3.3   Team OKR

The Team OKR are the goals and results that the team wants to achieve to meet the PMO OKR. These objectives are more focused and detailed, serving as input for the definition of actions that the team will perform.

The definition of these OKR is performed by the team itself with a three-month view. The objectives and expected outcomes are to be achieved and have the ambition to create challenges for the PMO team to work together and with clear and defined focus.

If during the definition of Team OKR there are already identified some actions, these should be noted and included in the team's backlog for further discussion during Sprint Planning.

3.4   Sprint Planning

Sprint Planning is the first meeting to begin Sprint. It is the moment of planning the actions that will be performed by the PMO team during the Sprint. In this case, it is suggested that the duration of Sprint is one month. This ceremony should be held with the whole team of the PMO, they will be responsible for knowing the team and ability to commit to the delivery of Sprint.

The main result of this event are the actions set to be held on Sprint beginning. One way to control these actions is to use a kanban [10], as presented in Fig. 2.

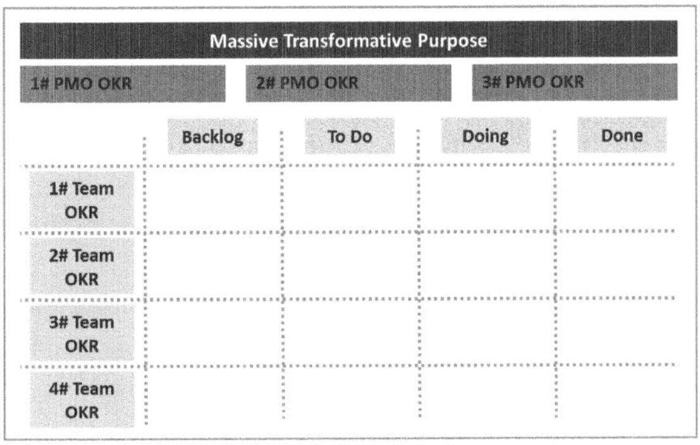

Fig. 2. Monitoring framework of the actions of Sprint. (Source: own authorship).

To determine what Sprint actions will be, the team must consider the actions that are already in their backlog and the actions they will propose to achieve Team OKRs. The actions that are selected must be moved or added in the "To Do" kanban column. An important point is that in this ceremony one should not focus on the details of how each action will be performed. It should be clear "What" will be done, the "How" can be detailed when any member of the team takes that action.

In order to conduct this and other Sprint ceremonies, the role of PO is performed by the PMO manager. The role of SM is performed by any team member who knows the methodology, except for the PO. The role of SM must be alternated between the members of the team anytime. it is suggested that the exchange occurs every three months. The exchange of members for the role of SM is important so that all team consolidate the understanding of the methodology facilitating in the moment of disseminating this knowledge.

3.5 Weekly Meeting

The Weekly Meeting is a meeting with all the PMO team. Its purpose is to monitor the actions. This meeting should take place in front of the team kanban and should take a maximum of 15 min.

Each team member should answer the three questions: What did I do last week? What will I do this week? Is there any impediment for completing my job?

This moment is important for the team to synchronize the activities being carried out and the main milestone for the kanban to be updated. Ideally, the update is performed as the actions are initiated (by moving tasks from "to do" to "doing" status) or completed (by moving tasks from "doing" to "done" status). If it does not, the actions must be updated at the most before the Weekly Meeting.

3.6 Sprint Review

This ceremony is the moment where the team presents its deliverables, the result of the completion of the actions defined for Sprint. All team members must participate and can also be of top management people invited to contribute feedback of deliveries made.

If any action has not been completed, it must return to the team's backlog. This action will be evaluated at the next Sprint, if it continues to be a priority compared to other backlog actions. In addition, the feedback obtained during the ceremony may generate new items in the backlog, which in turn will be evaluated together with the others in the Sprint Planning meeting.

At the end of the meeting, after deliveries have been submitted and with the feedback received, it is time to update the Team OKR and PMO OKR based on the result obtained in Sprint. In this moment, only the team participates and must be used to reflect on the evolution of its goals and the next challenges.

3.7 Sprint Retrospective

Sprint Retrospective is a time for the team to review how Sprint was going. This is an exclusive event for the PMO team member who participated in Sprint. This is the ceremony that ends Sprint.

It is the moment where it seeks to identify the positives and negatives that have occurred throughout the Sprint. For the positives, a collective agreement is created by the group in maintaining these attitudes, as well as defining improvement actions to be implemented in the next Sprint for points that are negative.

4   Discussion and Results

According to research conducted by VersionOne, 87% of companies that use the agile approach say their main benefit is their ability to manage with changing priorities [11]. This agility is essential considering the current market scenario that is constantly changing. For organizations to remain competitive they need to be agile to make changes and the PMO in this scenario becomes fundamental.

The PMO has the role of keeping the organization's strategy and its execution in line, as well as providing tools and techniques to support the organization in these transformations. Approximately 73% of the organizations surveyed by PMI, believed that one of the main tasks of the PMO is to provide standards for Project Management [4].

The use of agile approaches to project management has been steadily increasing to meet the need for changing organizational priorities. About 71% of organizations report that they use agile approaches to their projects sometimes, often and always [4].

Analyzing this context, as the PMO can be the reference in Project Management with Agile approaches, while he does not use this approach in their daily work? The model of performance proposed in this article comes in response to this questioning, providing the PMO with an agile approach to its operation. The use of this model evidences the pillars of the agile methods transparency, inspection and adaptation, making the PMO can be considered a PMO Agile.

5   Conclusion

This paper presented a model of action for a PMO Agile. The fact that companies are seeking market competitiveness, forces them to have the need to make changes, and the Agile PMO serves as support for them.

The proposed model may brings contributions to the community regarding agile practices applied to project management and innovative practices for agile businesses. The proposed model provides new techniques for PMO performance and can be widely used, thus contributing to the growth of new techniques for agile project management. In organizational transformations, the proposed model may contribute to the management of complexity as well as a support strategy to scale the agile in large organizations.

This model is currently used in the PMO of a private company in the region of Rio Grande de Sul. Its use in the first months has already shown benefits in terms of organization, transparency and focus of the PMO's performance in the organization. Based on reports from the team members themselves, there is an improvement in several points of daily life:

- Individuals and Interactions: from the implantation of the model weekly interactions are carried out to discuss the team objectives and activities, before this interaction occurred monthly or bimonthly;
- Response to change: changes occur more naturally, as the focus becomes on the OKRs and more on the activities;
- Partial and recurring deliveries: the team delivers smaller deliveries, collect feedback, and evolve;
- Transparency of work: Every team has visibility of what is being done and can contribute;
- Motivated individuals: the team knows where it wants to go and works in synergy to achieve the results.

As future work, it is expected to collect some more information throughout the year of 2017 and later be consolidated and disclosed to test the performance improvement of the PMO.

References

1. Project Management Institute (PMI): Um Guia do Conhecimento em Gerenciamento de Projetos - Guia PMBOK®. Project Management Institute, 5th edn., Pennsylvania (2013)
2. Berman, S.: Digital transformation: opportunities to create new business models. Strategy Leadersh. **40**(2), 16–24 (2012)
3. Ismail, S., Malone, M.S., Geest, Y.V.: Organizações exponenciais: por que elas são 10 vezes melhores, mais rápidas e mais baratas que a sua (e o que fazer a respeito). HSM Editora, São Paulo (2015)
4. Project Management Institute (PMI): Pulse of the Profession: 9th Global Project Management Survey. http://www.pmi.org/-/media/pmi/documents/public/pdf/learning/thought-leadership/pulse/pulse-of-the-profession-2017.pdf. Accessed 15 May 2017
5. Duggan, K.: Getting Started with Objectives & Key Results (OKRs). E-book. BetterWorks, Palo Alto (2015)
6. Wodtke, C.: Introduction to OKRs. O'Reilly Media, Sebastopol (2016)
7. Schwaber, K., Sutherland, J.: The Scrum Guide. http://www.scrumguides.org/docs/scrumguide/v2016/2016-Scrum-Guide-US.pdf. Accessed 21 Apr 2017
8. Scrum Alliance: The 2015 State of Scrum Report. https://www.scrumalliance.org. Accessed 15 Apr 2017
9. Crawford, J.K.: The Strategic Project Office: A Guide to Improving Organizational Performance. Marcel Dekker, New York (2001)
10. Ohno, T.: O sistema Toyota de produção: além da produção em larga escala. Bookman, Porto Alegre (1997)
11. VersionOne: The 10th Annual State of AgileTM Report. http://stateofagile.versionone.com. Accessed 10 Apr 2017

Conceptual Studies and Theoretical Foundations of Agile/Lean

Metamodel for Requirements Traceability and Impact Analysis on Agile Methods

Carlos Andrei Carniel(✉) and Raquel Aparecida Pegoraro(✉)

Federal University of Fronteira Sul, Chapecó, SC, Brazil
carlos.andreic@gmail.com, raquel.pegoraro@uffs.edu.br

Abstract. Requirements traceability is a requirements management activity used to identify relations between requirements and to enable the comprehension of its dependencies. In the agile development changes are normal and occur at any moment in the project, requirements are written in the format of user stories which have dependencies between them. These dependencies can be technical or related to the business being developed. Handling dependencies among requirements and impact analysis is a challenge due to the possibility of refactoring and maintenance caused by not analyzed changes. This paper aims to propose a metamodel that enables requirements traceability and impact analysis in agile methods. The proposed metamodel presents the following contributions: enable traceability analysis through the mapping of dependencies between user stories; (b) allow identification of dependencies between user stories and between tasks; (c) management of the evolution of requirements; (d) support on impact analysis of changes.

Keywords: Metamodel · Requirements traceability · Agile methods
User stories

1 Introduction

Requirements traceability is a technique used to identify the relationships between requirements, architecture, and system implementation [6,18]. The documentation generated by the requirements traceability enables the comprehension of the dependencies relations, and it is implemented using a set of links among the requirements that relate to one another, and among the components which implement the requirements.

In the agile development, the most used way of describing requirements is through user stories. Dependencies and relations also apply to user stories [8], which normally are implemented taking into account the business value order given by the customer and not the technical dependencies in terms of project construction. If the user stories are implemented without taking into account the order and dependency in which they are inserted, there might happen significative changes along the project which will lead to a high level of refactoring and consequently to rework and costs higher than planned [4].

© Springer International Publishing AG 2018
V. A. Santos et al. (Eds.): WBMA 2017, CCIS 802, pp. 105–117, 2018.
https://doi.org/10.1007/978-3-319-73673-0_9

Dealing with dependencies between requirements is a success factor in building a product which meets certain specifications and at the same time contributes so that the project is developed under the budget [15]. Another factor that motivates this research is that agile methods usually do not present tools or methods that deal with requirement dependencies [22] as well as they often lack of impact analysis of changes [15].

This paper presents a metamodel intended to help on requirements traceability on agile method projects through the mapping of dependencies between user stories. Section 2 presents requirements traceability concepts. Section 3 presents the proposed metamodel. In the Sect. 3.1 assumptions that guided the construction of the metamodel are identified. Section 3.2 discusses the built metamodel, an analysis of its relations and the correspondent assumptions. Section 4 compares the proposed metamodel with other existing ones. Finally, Sect. 5 concludes with considerations and future work.

2   Requirements Traceability in Agile Methods

Requirements traceability is defined as the ability to describe and track a requirement from its origin to its end, that is, throughout its specification and development, until its subsequent deployment and use [6].

Rossberg [24] highlights the benefits of adopting traceability management in a software project:

- Risk minimization: a consequence of the ability to estimate the impact of a change before it is done.
- Scope change control: change management throughout the development process.
- Reduced development costs: a result of reduced rework and consequent time savings.
- Increasing team productivity: keeps the team synchronized, decreasing the chance that the workload is directed only to a specific team member, aligning deadlines for completing tasks.
- Test coverage: tracking a requirement since its inception and highlighting its dependencies makes it easy to test before each delivery.
- Visibility: makes it easy to view flow and development processes for everyone involved.

Rossberg [24] also stresses the importance of research on traceability of requirements in agile methods. The author affirms that the main expected contributions in improving the techniques of representing the requirements, their relations and dependencies in agile projects are: the improvement in the quality of the development, a greater understanding of the product during the development and control of changes.

The traceability of requirements in agile methods is a recurring theme of research, as it is not yet properly used by developers, a problem that is described in [6,19,25]. A survey by Espinoza and Garbajosa [6], emphasizes that most of the traceability techniques used depend on characteristics of the traditional method of development and there is a gap in research on traceability methods independent of development models and that can be applied in agile methodologies.

In agile development, it is assumed that changes in requirements throughout software development should be considered as normal and are part of the process of product evolution. Among the most common reasons for changing requirements, it is worth noting, according to Sayão and Leite [25]:

– Unidentified needs at the beginning of the project;
– Changes in the context where the problem is inserted;
– Correction of errors detected by quality processes;
– New perspectives from stakeholders.

Such changes result in changes in the design architecture, in the code base and in tests suite, according to Sayão and Leite [25]. Traceability assists in tracking these changes so that all artifacts related to a requirement that has been changed are readjusted. Changes in requirements affect the system as a whole, as they are the starting point for defining architecture and deciding the order of implementation, guiding developers to the generation of test cases and validation with the user.

3   Proposed Metamodel

This work aims to propose a metamodel that enables the traceability of requirements and analysis of impact in agile methods. For the development of the proposal initially, the assumptions that guided the construction of the metamodel for traceability of requirements through the dependence between user stories and analysis of impact on agile methods were identified. Subsequently, the metamodel was constructed in order to meet the defined assumptions. In the next step, the proposed metamodel is analyzed in each of its relations and the corresponding assumptions are confirmed. Finally, the proposed metamodel is compared to other existing metamodels located in the literature review.

3.1   Assumptions Identified for the Metamodel Construction

In order to delimit the assumptions to be used in the construction of the metamodel, information regarding the requirements engineering activities were considered according to Pressman [17]. The characteristics of user stories have been identified in the literature, with Cohn [4,5], Ambler [1], and Rosenberg and Stephens [21] authors established on the subject. In addition, it was taken into account agile project management in accordance with the iterative and incremental development process of the agile Scrum and XP methods, which use user stories to represent requirements [20]. Scrum and XP methods were considered because 77% of agile software projects use these methods, according to *Version One* (2017) [23].

The set of assumptions defined to construct the proposed metamodel is presented below.

AS1 - Requirements are written in the format of user stories: a requirement which is specified in the format of a user story describes functionalities with business value to *stakeholders* [1,4,17,21].

AS2 - User stories are documented in a structured way: user stories have a documentation structure which makes it possible to identify information from requirements. This structure is generally written in the form [1,4,13]:

As a <stakeholder>,
I can <feature>,
so that <business value>.

AS3 - User stories have people with roles involved, called *stakeholders*: user stories are written, developed, and validated by team members, customers and other people called *stakeholders*, who have influence on the user stories and interest on the requirements [4]. The user stories do not contain technical information, since they are written with simple language terms, aiming to represent the user view [1,5,7,17]. In the agile Scrum method, the *stakeholder* is called *Product Owner*.

AS4 - User stories are written and developed along the iterations: iterations or *sprints* are time periods predefined by *stakeholders*, which determine which stories will be developed during the iteration. One or more iterations may be part of a *release*, which is a version of the product delivered to the customer and comprises a set of features. The list of user stories constantly evolves throughout the project [4,5,8,17,22].

AS5 - User stories can have dependencies between them: the dependencies can be related to the business or technical (project or implementation) [7,8,15,22].

AS6 - User stories generate tasks that may also have dependencies: user stories generate tasks to be developed in an iteration. Tasks are implementation activities, architecture, or testing that produce tangible results. Tasks are intrinsically related and may depend on each other. These dependencies occur between tasks from the same user story and between different story tasks [2,4,17,21].

AS7 - Changing a user story might impact other user stories: the impact can occur between requirements (business rules) and between components (projects related to system building, generating bugs). Technical changes can lead to code or architecture refactoring [4,22].

AS8 - Dependencies between user stories and between tasks may cause impact: User stories, as well as tasks, are intrinsically related to each other. These relationships can be dependencies that impact stories when there is a change. It is possible, through user analysis, to assign an impact intensity to the dependencies between stories and between tasks [4,22].

3.2   Metamodel

For the development of the proposed solution, orientations from the Object Management Group (2015) [16], which specifies standards for metamodels in UML notation, were followed. To explain how the assumptions have been met, all of the metamodel relations are presented. The complete metamodel can be visualized in Fig. 1.

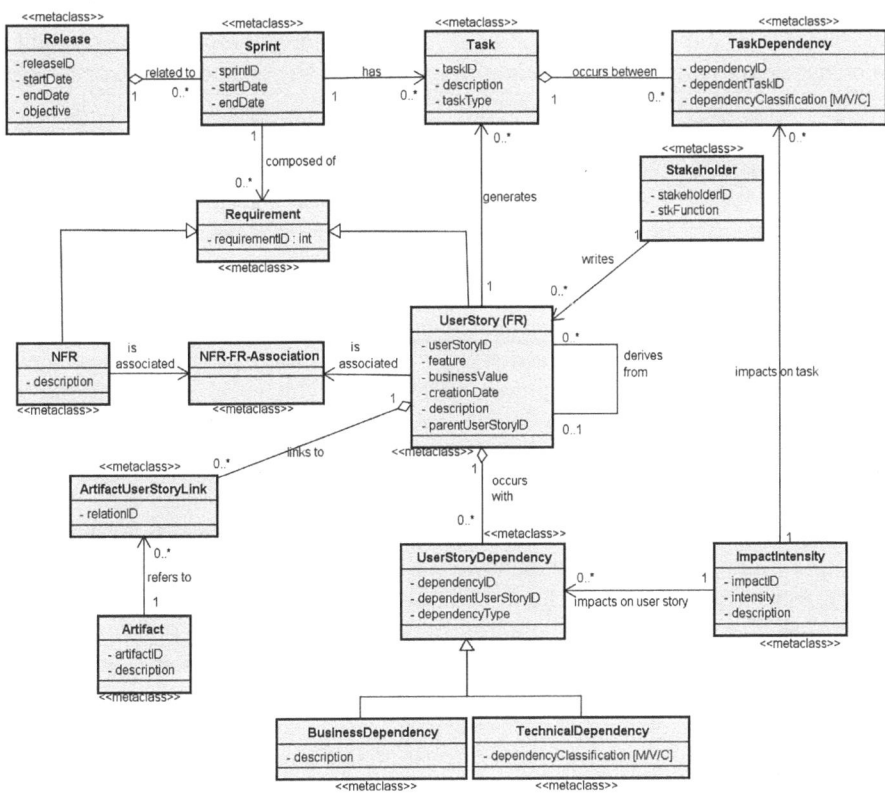

Fig. 1. Proposed metamodel for traceability of requirements in agile methods

User Stories, Their Textual Structure, and Stakeholders. The AS1 assumption states that the requirements are written in the form of user stories. In this way, the metamodel must be able to represent user stories describing its functionality and business value.

The AS2 assumption emphasizes that user stories are documented in a structured way and follow a textual pattern often used in agile methods. In this way, the metamodel must be able to store information about user stories and *stakeholders*, functionalities that should be developed in the story, and expected business value with story execution.

The AS3 assumption emphasizes that user stories have people and roles involved, called *stakeholders*. User stories are written from the perspective of these stakeholders and seek to meet their interests. As they are written to fit the user's vision, clear and easy-to-understand language is used, without specifying technical information. Thus, the metamodel should enable the user story relationship with *stakeholders* so that it is possible to manage roles and functions in a project.

Meeting the assumptions AS1 and AS2, the class *UserStory* was defined. This class presents the structure of a user story, with the attributes *userStoryID* (attribute identifier of each user story), *feature* (description of the functionality to be developed), and *businessValue* (description of the business value or benefit to be achieved with the development of the story).

Complementing the proposal, there is a need to distinguish between functional requirements (RF) and nonfunctional requirements (RNF). For this reason, the class *Requirement* was specialized in two other classes (*NFR* and *UserStory*). These two classes can be related through the association *NFR-FR-Association*.

Meeting the assumption AS3, the class *Stakeholder* was defined. This class presents the characteristics of a *stakeholder* in the metamodel. The *stakeholder* writes the user story and has a defined function related to the business value to be achieved with the development of the story. This class has the attributes *stakeholderID* and *stkFunction* (description of the *stakeholder* function in the system).

Development Along Iterations and User Stories Versioning. The AS4 assumption emphasizes that user stories are written and modified throughout the project iterations. Thus, the metamodel should allow the representation of changes in user stories throughout the iterations. To do this, user stories must be related to the iterations of which they are part, as well as iterations should be related to their corresponding *releases*. In addition, the metamodel must be able to represent versioning of user stories.

Meeting the assumption AS4, the class *UserStoryVersion* was defined. It presents the versioning of user stories, in order to represent changes between versions. *UserStoryVersion* is related to the classes *UserStory* and *Stakeholder*, that denote the *stakeholder* that made the change in the story. This class has the attributes *versionID*, *creationDate* (date the version was created), *description* (description of the change leading to the new version), *reason* (reason for changing the story) and *parentUserStoryID* (previous version of a user story to allow tracing story version).

Also considering the AS4 assumption, the classes *Sprint* and *Release* were defined. The *Sprint* class, related to the class *UserStory*, is intended to indicate which iteration a user story is bound to. This class has the attributes *sprintID* (iteration identifier attribute), *startDate* (iteration start date), and *endDate* (iteration end date). The Sprint class also relates to the Release class in order to express which release the iteration is bound to. *Release* has the following attributes: *releaseID*, *startDate*(release start date), *endDate* (Release end date) and *objective* (objective to be achieved with the development of *release* to be delivered to the client).

User Stories, Tasks and Artifacts Traceability. The AS5 assumption emphasizes that user stories may have dependencies on one another. These dependencies can be related to the business (referring to the order of execution, a situation where the most important stories are prioritized by the *stakeholder*) or techniques (software design and implementation). Thus, the metamodel must perform requirements traceability through links between user stories with dependent user stories, in addition to the link to related artifacts used for their implementation.

The AS6 assumption emphasizes that user stories generate tasks that may also have dependencies on each other. These dependencies can happen between tasks from the same story and tasks from different stories. Therefore, the metamodel must be able to perform traceability of dependencies through the link between tasks with dependent tasks.

Meeting the assumption AS5, the class *UserStoryDependency* was defined. This class is related to the *UserStory* class and has the following attributes: *dependencyID* (dependency identifier attribute), *dependentUserStoryID* (identifier of the dependent user story), and *dependencyType* (Type of dependency). The type of dependency was specialized in two other classes: *TechnicalDependency* (relative to technical dependency and having the *dependencyClassification* attribute, which classifies the dependencies in *M/V/C* (*Model/View/Controller*), which can be related to the database and architecture - *Model*, the interface *View*, and the code *Controller*) and *BusinessDependency* (which has the *description* attribute to describe the business dependency).

Meeting the assumption AS6, the *Task* class was constructed. This class is related to the class *UserStory* and describes the characteristics of a task generated from a user story. It has the following attributes: *taskID* (task identifier attribute), *description* (description of what should be done in the task) and *taskType* (task type - architecture, interface or code). Considering that tasks can also have dependencies on one another, the class *TaskDependency* has been defined. This class is related to the class Task and has the following attributes: *dependencyID*, *dependentTaskID*, and *dependencyClassification* (which classifies dependencies in *M/V/C*, as explained in the previous paragraph).

The metamodel also specifies the representation of relationships between user stories and artifacts through the *UserStoryArtifactLink* class. This class is related to the *UserStory* class and has the attribute *relationID*. Artifacts are represented by the Artifact class, which defines, for each artifact, an artifactID (artifact identifier attribute) and description (artifact description).

Impact of Dependencies and Changes. The AS7 assumption emphasizes that changing one user story can impact other user stories. These changes, if left untreated, can generate code or architecture refactoring. Thus, the metamodel must indicate, through the analysis of the user, what is the impact that a story or task that has dependency with another will cause if it is modified.

The AS8 assumption emphasizes that dependencies between user stories and between tasks can also have an impact. In this way, the metamodel should present a way to indicate, through the stakeholder analysis, what the impact would be between dependencies if any modification of the stories/tasks occurred.

Considering the assumptions AS7 and AS8, in order to represent the impact of dependencies between user stories and between tasks, in addition to determining the impact caused by a change, the class *ImpactIntensity* was defined. This class is related to the other three classes previously presented (*UserStoryVersion*, *UserStoryDependency* and *TaskDependency*) and has the attributes *impactID* (impact identifier), *intensity* (which assigns an intensity to the impact), and *description* (description about the impact). The impact prediction can be performed by analyzing the dependencies. In this way, one should carefully observe the tasks that were performed to develop the story. This analysis makes it possible to know if what was done in the tasks of past story will have an impact on the tasks of the current story being developed. The *intensity* attribute in the relationship between *ImpactIntensity* and *UserStoryDependency* along with *ImpactIntensity* and *TaskDependency*, seeks to measure how much the stories or tasks are dependent on one another and how much a story or task may be affected if the necessary corrections are not made after changes are made. In the relationship between *ImpactIntensity* and *UserStoryVersion*, the attribute *intensity* informs how much impact will be caused by a change that led to a new version of a story.

4   Comparison of the Metamodel with Existing Ones

This section presents a comparative table between the metamodels of traceability of requirements in the literature with the proposed metamodel. In order to compare the metamodels, it is necessary to define criteria based on expected attributes or functionalities of traceability models applied in the management of requirements. Lang and Duggan [12] lists a set of requirements that traceability models should be able to contemplate. Among them, we highlight the following:

- To register unique descriptions of all requirements;
- To classify the requirements into logical groups defined by the user;
- To specify requirements using textual, graphical, or model-based descriptions;
- To define traceable associations between requirements;
- To register and control changes and versions.
- To support cooperative work between members of a team;
- To support notation and modeling patterns.

Hoffmann et al. [9] also elaborates a set of desirable attributes for traceability models and requirements management:

- Support to changes and versioning of requirements;
- Requirements traceability support;
- To allow analysis of progress of requirements throughout the project;
- To allow interface with other tools and relate requirements of different models;

From the requirements presented by Lang and Duggan [12] and Hoffmann et al. [9] and based on the objectives of this work, aimed at the traceability of requirements in projects using agile methods, 10 criteria were identified in order to compare the models:

C1 - *Supports relationships with other documents*: allows one to relate artifacts or requirements with external documents related to stories and tasks.

C2 - *Supports textual representation of requirements*: allows the representation and storage of requirements in a way that they can be visualized textually.

C3 - *Supports vertical traceability*: allows traceability between requirements and different artifacts throughout development, that is, the traceability of relationships and dependencies.

C4 - *Supports horizontal traceability*: allows traceability of different versions of the same requirement or artifact at a given point in the project.

C5 - *Supports the representation of changes*: allows the representation of changes along the iterations.

C6 - *Supports impact representation*: allows the representation of impact of changes.

C7 - *Supports representation of impact of dependencies between user stories*: allows the representation of the impact of dependencies between stories and between tasks through the analysis of user stories.

C8 - *Supports versioning*: allows the representation and registering of the different versions of requirements (user stories) throughout the development.

C9 - *Supports the relationship of stakeholders to requirements and artifacts*: allows representing which *stakeholders* are directly involved with requirements or artifacts, in order to identify roles and attributions.

C10 - *Constructed aiming the application in agile methodologies*: specified in order to fit the phases of an agile software development project (releases, iterations, tasks) and how requirements are written through user stories.

The models compared are:

- **M1** - Ramesh's model [19]: This model focuses on the analysis of information related to agents, sources, and objects, considered as the three dimensions of traceability models.
- **M2** - Lang's model [12]: In this model, RMTool is presented, a prototype of a tool that controls and manages requirements in a multidisciplinary process, focusing on the characteristics that are not adequately addressed by commercial use tools.
- **M3** - Letelier's model [14]: This metamodel of traceability requirements designed in UML language aims to represent software artifacts and the relationships between requirements.

- **M4** - Briand's model [3]: This metamodel is built in UML notation and presents related diagrams that express the impact caused by changes in requirements. The purpose of this impact analysis is to identify what can be affected by a change and, based on this information, to keep the model current and consistent.
- **M5** - Kassab's model [11]: Built in UML notation, this metamodel aims to represent nonfunctional requirements, functional requirements and their relationships, each requirement being related to a phase of software development.
- **MP** - Metamodel proposed.

Thus, as shown in Table 1, the models were compared with respect to whether they meet the defined criteria.

The M1 model allows the association of artifacts and requirements with external documents, and thus meets criterion C1. This model also supports textual representation of requirements and vertical traceability, meeting the criteria C2 and C3. However, the model is not able to trace requirements horizontally, relating their different versions, and therefore, does not meet the C4 criterion. The model is still able to represent changes made to the requirements and define relationships with *stakeholders*, meeting criteria C5 and C9. However, it does not present any kind of representation of the impact of dependencies between requirements and between user stories, thus it does not meet criteria C6 and C7. Likewise, it does not allow to represent the versioning of the requirements and it is not focused on agile methodologies, therefore it does not cover the criterion C10.

The model M2 does not allow to relate the requirements with artifacts and in this way does not meet criterion C1. Nevertheless, this model supports the textual representation of the requirements, vertical and horizontal traceability and representation of changes, contemplating criteria C2, C3, C4, and C5. However, the M2 model does not support the representation of impact nor dependencies between user stories, it does not support versioning, nor has it been designed to be applied in agile software development projects, thus failing to criteria C6, C7, C8, and C10. However, it supports the relationship of *stakeholders* with requirements and artifacts, thus covering criterion C9.

In the same way as the M2 model, the M3 model does not consider the relationship of requirements with artifacts and, therefore, does not meet criterion C1. This model supports the textual representation of the requirements and implements both horizontal and vertical traceability, satisfying the C2, C3, and C4 criteria. Criterion C9 is also met since it is possible to relate *stakeholders* to requirements and artifacts. However, the M3 model does not allow the representation of changes, the impact of changes and between dependencies. Furthermore, it does not support versioning and was not designed to be suitable for agile methods. Therefore, it does not meet the criteria C5, C6, C7, C8, and C10.

The M4 model also does not allow the relationship of requirements to software artifacts and, unlike the models previously compared, it does not support the textual representation of requirements, thus not meeting criteria C1 and C2. As this model allows for vertical traceability, the representation of changes, impact of changes and versioning, the criteria C3, C5, C6, and C7 are met.

However, horizontal traceability, impact representation through dependencies between user stories, stakeholder relationships with requirements and artifacts, and appropriateness with agile software methods are not attributes presented by this model, which therefore does not meet the criteria C4, C7, C9, and C10.

The M5 model allows associating requirements with artifacts, enables the textual representation of requirements, vertical and horizontal traceability, and supports the relationship of *stakeholders* to requirements and artifacts, thus including criteria C1, C2, C3, C4, and C9. However, the M5 model does not support the representation of changes over iterations and their impact. In addition, the impact of dependencies between user stories and tasks is also not supported by the model, which, like the previously compared models, was not specified in order to meet the development process of agile methods. Thus, criteria C5, C6, C7, C8, and C10 are not met by the M5 model.

Finally, the metamodel proposed (MP) supports the relationship of user stories with artifacts, as mentioned in Sect. 3.2, thus meeting criterion C1. The MP also supports the textual representation of the requirements, since the class *UserStory* allows registration of attributes referring to user stories. In this way, the proposed metamodel contemplates criterion C2. In addition, MP supports vertical traceability, so that it is possible to relate different user stories and tasks and analyze their dependencies. The metamodel also supports horizontal traceability, and it is possible to represent the different versions of the same user story throughout the development. Thus, the proposed metamodel meets the C3 and C4 criteria. The MP also covers criterion C5, since through the different versions of the stories it is possible to verify what was modified and the reasons that led to the modification. Regarding the impact, the MP model supports both the impact representation caused by changes and the impact that can exist in the dependency between user stories, thus contemplating the C6 and C7 criteria. The model also supports the versioning of the stories, and the relationship of the stories with requirements and artifacts, thus meeting criteria C8 and C9. Finally, considering that the proposed metamodel was constructed with the purpose of attending agile methodologies that use user stories to represent requirements and that present an iterative and incremental development process, it can be stated that criterion C10 is met.

Table 1. Traceability models comparison

	C1	C2	C3	C4	C5	C6	C7	C8	C9	C10
M1	X	X	X		X				X	
M2		X	X	X	X				X	
M3		X	X	X					X	
M4		X		X	X		X			
M5	X	X	X	X					X	
MP	X	X	X	X	X	X	X	X	X	X

5   Conclusion and Future Work

This work presented a metamodel built to assist in the traceability of requirements in agile methods. The study of models and methods to represent dependencies between user stories and the impact analysis presents itself as a recurrent theme of research, given the need to manage changes in agile methods.

The metamodel was elaborated based on assumptions about user stories found in the literature. Subsequently, each assumption was analyzed with respect to the corresponding classes specified in the metamodel. The comparison of the proposed metamodel with other existing metamodels demonstrated that traceability models can be applied for different purposes.

Considering the analysis of the described results, it was observed that the work presents the following contributions: (a) An analysis of requirements traceability through dependency mapping between user histories; (b) The identification of dependencies between user stories and between tasks; (c) The visibility of the evolution of requirements; (d) The support in the impact analysis of changes.

Although a metamodel is essential for managing dependencies in agile methods, it is not enough. A tool is needed for populating the metamodel with user stories, tasks, and dependencies. To this end, a software visualization tool is being developed to represent the user stories and their dependencies so that the evolution of requirements and the impact of changes can be visualized.

References

1. Ambler, S.: Agile Modeling: Effective Practices for Extreme Programming and the Unified Process. Wiley, New York (2002)
2. Breitman, K., Leite, J.C.S.P.: Managing user stories. In: International Workshop on Time-Constrained Requirements Engineering (2002)
3. Briand, L.C., Labiche, Y., O'Sullivan, L.: Impact analysis and change management of UML models. In: Proceedings of the International Conference on Software Maintenance. ICSM, 22–26 September 2003. IEEE Computer Society, Washington, DC (2003)
4. Cohn, M.: User Stories Applied: For Agile Software Development. Addison-Wesley Professional, Boston (2004)
5. Cohn, M.: Succeeding with Agile: Software Development Using Scrum. Pearson Education, London (2010)
6. Espinoza, A., Garbajosa, J.: A study to support agile methods more effectively through traceability. Innovations Syst. Softw. Eng. 7, 53–69 (2011)
7. Gaur, V., Soni, A.: A novel approach to explore inter agent dependencies from user requirements. Procedia Technol. 1, 412–419 (2012)
8. Gomez, A., Rueda, G., Alarcón, P.P.: A systematic and lightweight method to identify dependencies between user stories. In: Sillitti, A., Martin, A., Wang, X., Whitworth, E. (eds.) XP 2010. LNBIP, vol. 48, pp. 190–195. Springer, Heidelberg (2010). https://doi.org/10.1007/978-3-642-13054-0_17
9. Hoffmann, M., Kuhn, N., Weber, M.: Requirements for requirements management tools. In: Proceedings of the 12th IEEE International Requirements Engineering Conference, pp. 301–308 (2004)

10. Kannenberg, A., Saiedian, H.: Why software requirements traceability remains a challenge. CrossTalk J. Def. Softw. Eng. **22**(5), 14–19 (2009)
11. Kassab, M., Ormandjieva, O., Daneva, M.: Traceability metamodel for change management of nonfunctional requirements. In: Proceedings of the 2008 Sixth International Conference on Software Engineering Research, Management and Applications. IEEE Computer Society, Washington, DC (2008)
12. Lang, M., Duggan, J.: A tool to support collaborative software requirements management. Requir. Eng. J. **6**, 161–172 (2001)
13. Leffingwell, D.: Agile Software Requirements: Lean Requirements Practices for Teams, Programs, and the Enterprise. Addison-Wesley Professional, Boston (2010)
14. Letelier, P.: A framework for requirements traceability in UML-based projects. In: Proceedings of the 1st International Workshop on Traceability in Emerging Forms of Software Engineering (TFFSE 2002) (2002)
15. Martakis, A., Daneva, M.: Handling requirements dependencies in agile projects: a focus group with agile software development practitioners. In: 2013 IEEE Seventh International Conference on Research Challenges in Information Science (RCIS). IEEE (2013)
16. Object Management Group: Unified Modeling Language Specification. UML 2.5 with Action Semantics, Final Adopted Specification (2015). www.omg.org
17. Pressman, R.S.: Software Engineering: A Practitioner's Approach. Palgrave Macmillan, New York (2005)
18. Ramesh, B., Powers, T., Stubbs, C., Edwards, M.: Implementing requirements traceability: a case study. In: Proceedings of the Second IEEE International Symposium on Requirements Engineering. IEEE (1995)
19. Ramesh, B., Jarke, M.: Toward reference models for requirements traceability. IEEE Trans. Softw. Eng. **27**, 58–93 (2001)
20. Sliger, M., Broderick, S.: The Software Project Manager's Bridge to Agility. Addison-Wesley Professional, Boston (2008)
21. Rosenberg, D., Stephens, M.: Extreme Programming Refactored: The Case Against XP. Apress, Berkeley (2008)
22. Trkman, M., Mendling, J., Krisper, M.: Using business process models to better understand the dependencies among user stories. Inf. Softw. Technol. **71**, 58–76 (2015)
23. Version One: 11th annual state of agile survey. Technical report, Version One (2017)
24. Rossberg, J.: Beginning Application Lifecycle Management. Apress, Berkeley (2014)
25. Sayão, M., Leite, J.C.S.P.: Rastreabilidade de requisitos. RITA 13.1 (2006)

Organizational Transformation and Cultural Aspects on Agile Business

For Some Places More Than Others - Agility and Organizational Culture

Lourenço P. Soares[1,2(✉)] and Ângela Freitag Brodbeck[2]

[1] ThoughtWorks Brasil, Porto Alegre, Brazil
lous@thoughtworks.com
[2] Universidade Federal do Rio Grande do Sul, Porto Alegre, Brazil
angela@brodbeck.com.br

Abstract. The adoption of agile methods for software development has proven to be an activity sensitive to the culture of the organizations seeking to adopt them. Agile projects occur in different situations: from the most ideal to those that require extensive adaptations. This study aims to explore the relationship between selected basic cultural assumptions of organizations and agile practices. Correlations identified were explored looking to offer an initial map suggesting approaches to introduce agile practices based on the cultural profile of the organization. The most notable results were that basic cultural assumptions of "Pragmatism", "Favors communication" and "Collegial/participative" are the ones most correlated with agile practices and the practices of "co-location", "Test Driven Development", "Continuous Integration", "Code refactoring", "pair programming" and "Stand-up meeting" showed no representative correlations with basic cultural assumptions, indicating that they may be a good alternative to start an agile adoption by technical practices. One of the main contributions of this work is proposing a preliminary model that highlights the relationship between organizational culture and adoption of agile practices, suggesting areas for further research.

Keywords: Organizational culture · Agile methodologies · Agile practices
Adoption of agile practices · Cultural dimensions · Basic assumptions
TDD · Continuous integration · Stand-up meeting · Co-location

1   Introduction

There are few companies these days that can remain competitive without Information Technology. Be it at the core of the business or limited to opportunistic explorations, IT projects can determine the success or failure of an organization. These projects are managed in many different ways, from ad hoc processes to the waterfall model using Gantt charts.

At the turn of century, noticing the chaos of the absence of a proper process and the frequent inefficiency of the waterfall model [1], a group of software developers proposed "agile" as a more appropriate way to manage IT projects [2]. Highsmith [3], one of the signatories of the Agile Manifesto [4] states that the growth and the criticism of agile

© Springer International Publishing AG 2018
V. A. Santos et al. (Eds.): WBMA 2017, CCIS 802, pp. 121–133, 2018.
https://doi.org/10.1007/978-3-319-73673-0_10

methods have to do with values and culture, and not taking cultural factors into account is the main cause of failure in the adoption of software development methodologies. Research by Begel and Nagappan [5] identified the incompatibility with culture as one of the barriers to adoption of agile methods.

In contrast, Robinson and Sharp [6] indicate that agile practices can be adapted to produce a methodology that is appropriate for a particular culture, and cultural analysis can help prepare an organization to introduce changes [7].

Often, there is a conflicting relationship between culture and practices that one seeks to adopt in IT organizations, which can harm change initiatives, particularly in the context of agile methodologies adoption. Thus, this study aims to:

(a) Identify in literature how the various characteristics of an organizational culture are described and how they can be measured;
(b) Identify the practices that best represent, for the purposes of this work, the principles behind agile methodologies;
(c) Identify which basic assumptions of organizational culture are more or less related to the adoption of agile practices by mapping the basic assumptions prevailing in organizational culture of different companies and their correlation with the adoption of agile practices in the implementation of information systems in said companies.

2   Main Elements of Study Execution

This study was based on cultural elements that can be classified as national, regional, organizational, group or individual, focusing on organizational elements. Besides these, elements of agile methods and its main practices were analyzed and mapped.

2.1   Culture Elements

Ali and Brooks [8] define culture as "shared patterns of behavior." Within the organization, the definition by Ed Schein, also used by Fleury et al. [9] was used:

> The culture of a group can now be defined as a pattern of shared basic assumptions learned by a group as it solved its problems of external adaptation and internal integration, which has worked well enough to be considered valid and, therefore, to be taught to new members as the correct way to perceive, think, and feel in relation to those problems [10].

Both Hofstede and Hofstede [11] and Schein [10] suggest the use of different dimensions to describe an organizational culture in aspects relevant to empirical studies. For Schein basic assumptions are organized in the following dimensions [12]:

Nature of Human Activity: Between *Environment dominant* (the organization acts as if subordinate to the environment it operates) and *Organization dominant* (the organization believes in its ability to determine the environment and the market). Between *Proactive* (the organization accepts that individuals can cause instability in the search for improvement) and *Reactive/fatalistic* (the organization expects the protocol to be followed and when unforeseen results happen, it accepts the consequences).

Nature of Reality and Truth: Between *Moralistic authority* (the organization trusts the boss/expert/manual to determine the proper way of doing things) and *Pragmatism* (the organization tries to obtain objective information and believes truth emerges from the exchange of ideas among all).

Nature of Space: Between *Favors privacy* (the organization creates private spaces and discloses information as needed) and *Favors communication* (the organization adopts an environment that facilitates the rapid exchange of ideas).

Nature of Time: Between *Near future oriented* (the organization uses its planning as basis for decisions) and *Past oriented* (the organization revisits previous experiences to look for solutions to problems). Between *Long time units* (organization favors a long-term view, disregards minor delays) and *Short time units* (the organization plans its activities with a short horizon of time and sees small delays as significant).

Nature of Human Nature: Between *Humans are basically good* (the organization believes that properly motivated people will exceed expectations) and *Humans are basically evil* (the organization suspects that people will act inappropriately if given the chance). Between *Human nature is fixed* (the organization believes that people are what they are and cannot change) and *Human nature is mutable* (the organization believes that people adapt to different situations and can improve depending on the context).

Nature of human relationships: Between *Groupism* (the organization believes that all good things come from the group and strive to create consensus) and *Individualism* (the organization believes that individual talent is key to problem solving). Between *Collegial/participative* (authority is determined by the context and the leader defers to the group) and *Authoritarian/paternalistic* (the organization believes in a strong hierarchy).

2.2   Elements of Agile Methods

The Agile Manifesto [4] and the methodologies associated with it caused a significant change in the way teams develop software. According to Taylor [13]:

> Agile methodologies generally promote a project management process that encourages frequent inspection and adaptation, a leadership philosophy that encourages teamwork, self-organization and accountability, a set of engineering best practices that allow for rapid delivery of high-quality software and a business approach that aligns development with customer needs and company goals.

Fowler [29] points out that "one of the hardest parts of introducing agile methods into an organization is the cultural change it causes." Because of the flexible nature of agile methodologies, it is often better to adapt practices when these prove inadequate to a given context, provided the agile values are respected [2, 6, 14, 15].

In order to compare practices and adoption, a number of agile practices were selected based on a comparison of several authors [2, 5, 14, 16–20] (Table 1). They were selected by measuring how often they were mentioned in the reference literature and mapping them according to the 12 principles of the Agile Manifesto [4] (the principle of "Our highest priority is to satisfy the customer..." was considered as a meta principle, resulting of the conjunction of the others and as a guiding principle for the application of all practices, not mapping exclusively to a single practice).

Table 1. List of selected Agile practices and its corresponding principles. Number of papers considered that reference the practice in parenthesis.

Practices (mentions)	Reference	Principles
Delivery planning (5)	PLAN	Welcome changing requirements...
Requirements in form of stories (3)	REQS	
Iterations/small, frequent deliveries (7)	ITER	Deliver working software frequently...
Active customer involvement (7)	CUST	Business people and developers must work together...
Multidisciplinary team (2)	MULT	
Motivation (2)	MOTV	Build projects around motivated individuals...
Co-location (2)	COLO	The most efficient (...) face-to-face conversation
Test Driven Development (8)	TDDV	Working software is the primary measure...
Continuous Integration (8)	CINT	
Sustainable pace (6)	PACE	Agile processes promote sustainable development...
Code refactoring (6)	REFA	Continuous attention to technical excellence...
Pair programming (7)	PAIR	
Simplicity (5)	SIMP	Simplicity...
Incremental project (2)	INCR	
Minimum modeling/documentation (2)	MIND	
Collective understanding (7)	COLU	The best (...) designs emerge from self-organizing teams
Stand-up meeting (3)	STND	
Visual progress indicators (4)	VIND	
Retrospectives/learning (3)	RETR	At regular intervals, the team reflects...

3   Study Method

This work is understood as exploratory study [21]. At the time the survey was performed, no other studies were found relating cultural dimensions and agile practices adoption.

This study used a quantitative research method [22], using as instrument an online survey form. It was considered, according to literature [10, 11], to be good enough for an initial search of insights into the role of culture in inhibiting or facilitating organizational change.

The case study was carried out between March and April of 2011 in the company ThoughtWorks Inc., global leader in consulting and the use of Agile methodologies in implementation of software development projects [23]. The source data was collected from ThoughtWorks Inc. consultants delivering software or providing advice on software delivery based on their experience during the delivery or after it has finished. These consultants were distributed globally in many different organizations and cultures, which have different levels of knowledge of Agile.

For cultural dimensions, the model used was adapted from the one proposed by Schein [12] described in Sect. 2.1. A five point scale between the cultural assumptions at each end of a given dimension was used to measure an organization's manifested behavior with regards to that dimension.

A comparative analysis of previous works was used for the selection of agile practices surveyed (Table 1). The adoption of a given practice was measured using the scale proposed by Boehm and Turner [24] for "Levels of Software Method Understanding and Use" (Table 2).

Table 2. Levels of software method understanding and use.

Level	Description
Level -1	May have technical skills, but unable or unwilling to collaborate or follow shared methods
Level 1B	With training, able to perform procedural method steps
Level 1A	With training, able to perform discretionary method steps
Level 2	Able to tailor a method to fit a precedented new situation
Level 3	Able to revise a method (break its rules) to fit an unprecedented new situation

The responses were based on the subjective perception of consultants from Thought-Works Inc. on the client's experience and satisfaction with agile methods; the culture of the client organization; and the understanding and use of agile methods put forward by employees of the organization at the end of the project.

For data analysis, descriptive and multivariate statistical procedures were employed using statistical functions as Pearson correlation and hypothesis test (t test error probability Type I (α) accepted of 0.01) [25–27]. No data cleansing process was performed. Each dimension of culture was separated in the two basic assumptions it corresponds to, with assumptions on the left of the scale having the negative correlation value, and assumptions on the right of the scale having the positive correlation value. Thus, negative correlations between a practice and a dimension indicate, in fact, a direct correlation with the assumption on the left in a certain cultural dimension. To avoid drawing conclusions on extreme situations with a low number of responses, only the top 20% of the assumption and practice pairs with the highest correlation were selected for analysis [13].

4   Analysis of Results

The survey consisted of questionnaires distributed to a population of 1400 consultants, with a return rate of 8.14% (114 responses), which allowed calculation of a correlation between the cultural dimensions researched and selected agile practices. The questionnaires were validated by two specialists from ThoughtWorks and the results verified and commented by five others. Both questionnaire and results were reviewed by three members on an examination board. The results can be seen in Table 3. The darker the

Table 3. Map of the correlation between practices and cultural dimensions.

Practices (Reference in Table 1)	Environment dominant → Organization dominant	Proactive → Reactive/fatalistic	Moralistic authority → Pragmatism	Favors privacy → Favors communication	Near future oriented → Past oriented	Long time units → Short time units	Humans are basically good → Humans are basically evil	Human nature is fixed → Human nature is mutable	Groupism → Individualism	Collegial/participative → Authoritarian/paternalistic
PLAN	0,0578	**0,4233**	**0,4362**	**0,3699**	0,2518	0,1772	**0,4088**	0,0438	0,1982	**0,4590**
REQS	0,1591	0,2092	0,3400	0,3332	0,2405	0,0515	0,1742	0,2145	0,3033	**0,3520**
ITER	0,1494	**0,4451**	**0,3814**	0,2531	0,1768	,0140	**0,4144**	0,0609	0,0848	0,3022
CUST	0,0614	**0,3764**	**0,4178**	**0,4326**	0,1178	0,0528	**0,4955**	0,3452	0,1751	**0,3813**
MULT	0,1268	0,1566	0,2876	0,3104	0,1620	0,0156	0,2419	0,2609	**0,3674**	0,3361
MOTV	0,0924	**0,4077**	**0,4707**	**0,3840**	0,1633	0,0261	**0,5151**	0,2859	0,2716	**0,4349**
COLO	0,0933	0,1612	0,2235	0,2871	0,0955	0,0988	0,3396	0,1935	0,1233	0,2527
TDDV	0,1785	0,0787	0,1787	0,0939	0,1686	0,1747	0,1309	0,0960	0,2463	0,2139
CINT	0,1001	0,1864	0,1428	0,0964	0,2848	0,1218	0,1677	0,0276	0,1656	0,1809
PACE	0,1152	0,2627	**0,3881**	0,3031	0,0218	0,0932	0,2931	0,2706	0,2961	0,2848
REFA	0,0236	0,1775	0,2552	0,1582	0,0469	0,0485	0,2506	0,1642	0,1586	0,2092
PAIR	0,1198	0,2237	0,1950	0,2899	0,1532	0,1033	0,2398	0,2499	0,1796	0,3226
SIMP	0,1149	0,3330	0,2517	**0,3791**	0,1446	0,0701	**0,3686**	0,2827	0,2453	**0,4057**
INCR	0,1122	0,2733	0,1849	0,2393	0,1589	0,1834	0,3195	0,1962	0,2312	**0,4253**
MIND	0,2079	0,2834	0,3052	**0,4489**	0,1682	0,0017	**0,3626**	0,2177	0,2900	**0,4686**
COLU	0,1373	**0,3687**	,4271	**0,4221**	0,1198	0,1067	**0,4515**	0,3250	**0,4153**	**0,5238**
STND	0,0709	0,0533	0,1778	0,2507	0,1013	0,0831	0,2499	0,1376	0,2340	0,2589
VIND	0,2309	0,2252	**0,3512**	**0,3755**	0,3043	0,0371	0,2999	0,1438	0,2138	0,3306
RETR	0,1840	0,1112	**0,3902**	**0,3941**	0,0981	0,1143	0,2353	0,1519	0,3413	0,2780

cell the higher the correlation, either positive or negative. It is important to notice that a high value for modular correlation does not imply that this correlation is significant. This requires a hypothesis test, which was done in selected cases.

Positive or negative correlations represent the influence of different assumptions on the adoption of a practice. In Table 3 cultural dimensions are in columns, so negative values indicate a strong correlation with assumptions to the left in the column heading while positive values indicate a strong correlation with assumptions to the right in the column heading. Only the highest 20% of the correlation results (in bold in Table 3) were selected for a detailed analysis. All correlations highlighted proved significant.

Based on the results, it is worth noting that the basic assumptions of "Pragmatism", "Favors communication" and "Collegial/participative" are the ones that correlate more with agile practices, with 8 practices with high correlation for each assumption. This can be seen as aligned with the four values of the Agile Manifesto [4] as seen in Table 4.

Table 4. Values of the agile manifesto and basic cultural assumptions.

Individuals and interactions over processes and tools	"Favors communication"
Working software over comprehensive documentation	"Pragmatism"
Customer collaboration over contract negotiation	"Collegial/participative", "Favors communication"
Responding to change over following a plan	"Pragmatism"

On the other hand, four dimensions showed no correlation among the 20% analyzed: Between "Environment dominant" and "Organization dominant"; Between "Near future oriented" and "Past oriented"; Between "Long time units" and "Short time units"; and between "Human nature is fixed" and "Human nature is mutable". It is surprising that the last one showed no correlation, since the concept of "Agile Mindset" [28] speaks explicitly about the belief that people can change.

Another interesting observation is that the practices of "co-location", "Test Driven Development", "Continuous Integration", "Refactoring code", "Pair programming" and "Stand-up meeting" showed no representative correlation with any basic assumption. This suggests that these practices are more culture "agnostic" and possibly can be adopted more easily by any organization. Many of these practices ("Test Driven Development", "Continuous Integration", "Refactoring code" and "Pair programming") are highly technical, which may explain why many adoptions of agile methodologies in organizations are led by software development teams.

Therefore, one could assume that, particularly in organizations with predominantly "Favors privacy", "Moralistic authority" and "Authoritarian/paternalistic" cultural assumptions, an Agile adoption will be more successful if it starts by implementing the practices of "co-location", "Test Driven Development", "Continuous Integration", "Refactoring code", "Pair programming" and "Stand-up meeting".

5   Conclusions and Contributions

Based on the highlighted correlations, one can argue that it was possible to identify cultural assumptions that are related to the adoption of agile practices. This was achieved by seeking in literature instruments which allow the classification of the culture of an organization, listing a set of practices representative of agile principles and looking to measure the correlations between these in real situations.

Although the results are encouraging, one must be aware that their validity is limited due to the inherent limitations and biases of surveys and the small number of responses. It is also a subjective matter within a fairly homogeneous population, limiting extrapolation of results.

Therefore it is considered that this work may contribute to a deeper exploration of the theme by suggesting significant correlations between the adoption of agile practices and cultural assumptions of different organizations.

To the academia, this work serves as an initial model to look into agile methods and practices in the organizational culture domain. We hope that these results encourage researchers to consider organizational culture as an important aspect in studies of adoption of these methodologies. For practitioners, we hope this inspire companies looking to adopt agile methodologies to consider the culture of its organization, and plan strategy accordingly, aiming, for example, to start the journey by the practices that seem less sensitive to culture, and eventually seeking to adapt their culture (or the expected results) according to these limitations.

Several possibilities for future studies arise from this work. To confirm its results, and mitigate any bias that this study could have been subject of, it is necessary to expand the set of sources analyzed, seeking a greater volume and diversity of data. In addition, a longitudinal study with a limited set of customers observing the impact of agile practices in organizational culture can help to establish a causal relationship and deepen the understanding of the nexus between agile practices and organizational culture. We believe it is also important that the practitioners of agile methodologies - from beginners to the more experienced - pay attention to day-to-day moments where culture was an impediment to improvement, or, to the contrary, a boost to change. Conveniently, the Agile Manifesto itself suggests moments of reflection where this debate can be rewarding.

Appendix A – Survey Questionnaire

Culture and Agile Practices
Please answer the questions below based on your experience in past and present ThoughtWorks projects you've been involved. Your name and the client/project information will be kept private and used only for data aggregation and to calculate response rate. Please feel free to leave feedback, remarks or describe a case of particular interest in the field available at the end of the form. Thanks for your time!

Project profile
The next few questions will be used to identify the project characteristics for aggregate analysis:

Client/project:	Your role:
Client country of origin:	Project end date:
Project type (Onshore / Offshore):	Project duration:

Client's experience with Agile: No experience 1 2 3 4 5 Experienced practitioners
Client's satisfaction with Agile: Extremely frustrated 1 2 3 4 5 Extremely satisfied
Did the project finish on target and on budget? Yes/No/Not finished/I don't know

Client Organization Culture
For the following questions, please answer what, in your opinion, best reflects the attitudes, behaviors and beliefs of the group involved in the project from the client's side.

Nature of Human Activity – 1. Does the organization acts as if dominated by the environment it is part of, trying to find available niches and considering all external factors before doing anything (e.g.: they refuse to make any changes without consulting every stakeholder, like legal and design people)? Or the organization believes in its capacity to influence the market with their own effort, displaying a belief in progress regardless of what the current consensus is (e.g.: they try and release products they believe in, regardless of marketing surveys)?

Environment dominant 1 2 3 4 5 Organization dominant

Nature of Human Activity – 2. Does the organization let its members act pro-actively and improve things even if it means making the environment unstable for everyone else sometimes (e.g.: They try many physical lay-outs until they find the one that is acceptable for everyone)? Or the organization expects its members to follow detailed instructions and act according to protocol, accepting their fate if something unexpected happens and the protocol breaks down (e.g.: They avoid updating their tech stack without many meetings and a detailed timeline)?

Pro - active 1 2 3 4 5 Reactive, fatalistic

Nature of Reality and Truth. Does the organization trusts the boss, local specialist or "the right way of doing things" to determine what is right when it is time to make a decision amid great uncertainty (e.g.: there is a methodology book that every one regards as the final arbitrator of any dispute)? Or the organization try to gather objective information and, in lack of those, believes that truth will come out of debate among everyone involved (e.g.: to make a decision, two or more members of the team explain their ideas and test it out to see what works best)?

Moralistic Authority 1 2 3 4 5 Pragmatism

Nature of Space. Does the organization adopts a working environment that favors private conversation, avoiding disrupting anybody with conversations that are not pertinent to the whole group, and only releasing information in a need-to-know basis (e.g.: the boss have people come to his office when he wants to talk to them and interrupting a colleague without permission is an offense)? Or the organization adopts a working environment that makes the fast exchange of ideas easy at the expense of individual privacy (e.g.: the team – including the boss – shares a common working area and the group is all facing the centre of the room when possible)?

Allowing privacy 1 2 3 4 5 Allowing communication

Nature of Time – 1. Is the organization normally focused in the near future, using a quarterly or annual goal as benchmark for decision-making (e.g.: they postpone a change until after the current release in order to avoid risking it)? Or the organization normally looks to past experiences when looking for solutions for a problem (e.g.: they do not adopt a given methodology because they tried before and it didn't work)? An intermediate position would be focus on the task at hand, without looking into long-term consequences or previous experiences.

Near future orientation 1 2 3 4 5 Past orientation

Nature of Time – 2. Does the organization favors a long term vision (months or years) and don't worry too much about small delays (e.g.: they are fine with a complex task taking longer than expected and are willing to negotiate the consequent delay in order to do the right thing). Or the organization plan activities with a short time frame (days or weeks) and consider small delays a big issue (e.g.: holding weekly status meetings where every delay is immediately looked into)?

Long time units 1 2 3 4 5 Short time units

Nature of Human Nature – 1. Does the organization believes that people are intrinsically good and, when properly motivated, will exceed expectations when performing the tasks they are responsible for (e.g.: they do not demand results, focusing on making sure everyone has all the resources necessary to do the job)? Or the organization believes people is intrinsically bad and believe people will misbehave if given the opportunity (e.g.: an organization that has cameras everywhere to make ensure security and good behavior)?

Humans are basically good 1 2 3 4 5 Humans are basically evil

Nature of Human Nature – 2. Does the organization believe that people are what they are and can't change their nature regardless of any context changes (e.g.: the organization prefers to postpone a meeting then let someone represent somebody else that is out sick)? Or the organization believes people can change, adapting to different roles depending on the situation and/or the way they are treated (e.g.: the organization lets a user pair with a developer if the user believes he can help that way)?

Human nature is fixed 1 2 3 4 5 Human nature is malleable

Nature of Human Relations – 1. Does the organization believes that all good things come from the group and members strive for conformity (e.g.: people frequently ask everybody else's opinion before deciding on trivial things)? Or the organization believes that individual talent is the solution for any problem (e.g.: if somebody works all night alone to do a nasty hack to fix an issue in production, then he or she is praised as an example)?

Group as center 1 2 3 4 5 Individual as center

Nature of Human Relations – 2. Is the authority in the organization determined by context, with the boss deferring to the group members' experience to assign power according to the situation (e.g.: the input of skilled engineers holds more weight in the decisions regarding the tech stack)? Or the organization believes in a strong hierarchy where power and influence are a consequence of each person's relative status (e.g.: no matter how obvious a solution is, it must be cleared with the boss first)?

Collegial/Participative 1 2 3 4 5 Authoritarian/paternalistic

	May have technical skills but unable or unwilling to collaborate or follow shared methods	With training, able to perform procedural method steps	With training, able to perform discretionary method steps	Able to tailor a method to fit a precedented new situation	Able to revise a method (break its rules) to fit an unprecedented new situation
Release planing					
Use of stories					
Frequent releases					
Client participation					
Morale					
Colocation					
TDD					
CI					
Sustainable pace					
Refactoring					
Whole team					
Pair Programming					
Simple design					
Incremental design					
Minimal documentation					
Shared understanding					
Stand-ups					
Information Radiators					
Retrospective/self-improvement					

Agile practices adoption
In the table below, please check the option that matches your perception of the client's team skill level in each given practice in the last day of the project.

Agile practices mastery levels
If a particular practice wasn't tried/does not apply in the project you are describing or the scale doesn't fit, leave that row unanswered. Mastery levels based on Cockburn (2000), Boehm and Turner (2003) and Sato et al. (2006).

References

1. Royce, W.: Software Project Management: A Unified Framework. Addison-Wesley Professional, Reading (1998)
2. Parsons, D., Ryu, H., Lal, R.: The impact of methods and techniques on outcomes from agile software development projects. In: McMaster, T., Wastell, D., Ferneley, E., DeGross, Janice I. (eds.) TDIT 2007. IIFIP, vol. 235, pp. 235–249. Springer, Boston, MA (2007). https://doi.org/10.1007/978-0-387-72804-9_16
3. Highsmith, J.: Agile Software Development Ecosystems. Addison-Wesley, Boston (2002)
4. Beck, K., Beedle, M., van Bennekum, A., et al.: Manifesto for Agile Software Development. In: Agilemanifesto.org (2017). http://agilemanifesto.org. Accessed 15 June 2017
5. Begel, A., Nagappan, N.: Usage and perceptions of agile software development in an industrial context: An exploratory study. In: International Symposium on Empirical Software Engineering and Measurement, vol. 1, pp. 255–264 (2007)
6. Robinson, H., Sharp, H.: XP culture: Why the twelve practices both are and are not the most significant thing. In: Agile Development Conference, vol. 1, pp. 12–21 (2003)
7. Dubé, L., Robey, D.: Software stories: three cultural perspectives on the organizational practices of software development. Acc. Manage. Inf. Technol. **9**, 223–259 (1999)
8. Ali, M., Brooks, L.: A situated cultural approach for cross-cultural studies in IS. J. Enterp. Inf. Manage. **22**, 548–563 (2009)
9. Fleury, M.T., Shinyashiki, G., Stevanato, L.A.: Entre a antropologia e a psicanálise: dilemas metodológicos dos estudos sobre cultura organizacional. Revista de Administração **32**, 23–37 (1997)
10. Schein, E.: Organizational Culture and Leadership. Jossey-Bass, San Francisco (2010)
11. Hofstede, G., Hofstede, G.J.: Cultures and Organizations: Software for the Mind. McGraw-Hill, New York (2004)
12. Schein, E.: Organizational Culture. Working paper (Sloan School of Management) (1988). 2088-88
13. Taylor, P.: The Lazy Project Manager. Infinite Ideas, Oxford (2009)
14. Sato, D., Bassi, D., Bravo, M., et al.: Experiences tracking agile projects: an empirical study. J. Braz. Comput. Soc. **12**, 45–64 (2006)
15. Cockburn, A.: Agile Software Development. Addison-Wesley Professional, Reading (2001)
16. Beck, K., Andres, C.: Extreme Programming Explained. Addison-Wesley Professional, Reading (2004)
17. Rumpe, B., Schröder, A.: Quantitative survey on extreme programming projects. In: International Conference on Extreme Programming and Flexible Processes in Software Engineering, vol. 3, pp. 26–30 (2002)
18. Forrester Research: Agile Development: Mainstream Adoption Has Changed Agility (2010)

19. Krebs, W.: Turning the knobs: A coaching pattern for XP through agile metrics. In: Wells, D., Williams, L. (eds.) XP/Agile Universe 2002. LNCS, vol. 2418, pp. 60–69. Springer, Heidelberg (2002). https://doi.org/10.1007/3-540-45672-4_7

20. Williams, L., Layman, L., Krebs, W.: Extreme Programming Evaluation Framework for Object-Oriented Languages, v. 1.4. Department of Computer Science, North Carolina State University (2004)

21. Yin, R.: Case Study Research: Design and Methods. Sage, Thousand Oak (2008)

22. Severino, A.: Metodologia do trabalho científico. Cortez, São Paulo (2002)

23. Palmer, L., Lawler, J.: Agile methodology in offshore outsourcing. J. Bus. Case Stud. **1**, 35–46 (2005)

24. Boehm, B., Turner, R.: Rebalancing your organization's agility and discipline. In: Maurer, F., Wells, D. (eds.) XP/Agile Universe 2003. LNCS, vol. 2753, pp. 1–8. Springer, Heidelberg (2003). https://doi.org/10.1007/978-3-540-45122-8_1

25. Schmuller, J.: Statistical Analysis with Excel For Dummies. Wiley, San Francisco (2009)

26. Chatman, J., Jehn, K.: Assessing the relationship between industry characteristics and organizational culture: how different can you be? Acad. Manag. J. **37**, 522–553 (1994)

27. Prajogo, D., McDermott, C.: The relationship between total quality management practices and organizational culture. Int. J. Oper. Prod. Manage. **25**, 1101–1122 (2005)

28. Rising, L.: The Power of an Agile Mindset (2011)

29. Fowler, M.: Using an agile software process with offshore development. In: Martinfowler.com (2006). http://www.martinfowler.com/articles/agileOffshore.html. Accessed 15 June 2017

Agile Practices and Future Trends, Evolution and Revolution (Technical or Managerial)

A Study on the Perception of Researchers About the Application of Agile Software Development Methods in Research

Nelson Marcelo Romero Aquino(✉), Adolfo Gustavo Serra Seca Neto,
and Heitor Silvério Lopes

Federal University of Technology - Paraná, Av. Sete de Setembro,
3165 - Rebouças CEP, Curitiba 80230-901, Brazil
nmarceloromero@gmail.com, {adolfo,hslopes}@utfpr.edu.br

Abstract. Papers on Agile Software Development methods are often focused on their applicability in commercial projects or organizations. There are no current studies that we know about addressing the application of these methods in research projects. The objective of this work is to describe the perception of researchers on the application of agile software development practices and principles for research projects. A study was conducted by constructing and applying a questionnaire to Brazilian researchers of different affiliations, formation and research areas in order to obtain information about their knowledge and openness to follow agile software development principles and practices.

Keywords: Agile software development methods
Software for research projects

1 Introduction

Since the arrival of Agile Software Development (ASD) approaches, the research community has been pursued to analyze their applicability in commercial environments, projects or organizations. Some works regarding this field of study are based on comparing traditional development methods with ASD [1], others seek to study the challenges derived from the application of agile processes in traditional organizations [2] or the suitability of using ASD methods to particular environments [3,4]. To the best of our knowledge, no research has been published to evaluate the application of ASD methods and practices in research projects within universities or the openness of the researchers to apply them to projects in which it is necessary to develop some kind of software.

The objective of this work is to describe researchers knowledge regarding ASD and their openness to follow agile software development principles and practices in research projects. For this purpose, data was collected from Brazilian researchers from different backgrounds by applying a questionnaire divided in several parts, each one regarding a concrete aspect such as the agreement with the agile principles or the knowledge about agile methods.

© Springer International Publishing AG 2018
V. A. Santos et al. (Eds.): WBMA 2017, CCIS 802, pp. 137–145, 2018.
https://doi.org/10.1007/978-3-319-73673-0_11

This work is organized as follows: Sect. 2 presents related works. Section 3 describes details about the construction of the questionnaire and its application. Section 4 presents the results obtained and explores their implications. Section 5 contains the conclusion and final discussions derived from this work.

2   Related Work

Although there are no works regarding the application of ASD in research projects in particular, several papers address their application in commercial environments. In [5], the perception of the impact of agile methods when deployed in a very large software development environment was evaluated, mainly from the viewpoint of agile transformation. The work applied a questionnaire on a population consisting of more than 1000 respondents working at Nokia from seven different countries in Europe, North America, and Asia. Among the respondents, 90% represented the Research and Development (R&D) area. The work concludes that ASD received very positive feedback. In the work presented by [6], a survey regarding the adoption of ASD from Finnish software practitioners was conducted, gathering answers from 408 persons representing 200 different organizations. Results show that most respondents were using ASD methods and that they are often adopted in order to increase the productivity and quality of the products and services. The study also concludes that the most common reasons preventing the adoption of ASD methods are lack of knowledge and a too traditionalist culture within an organization. The work by [7] addresses the knowledge regarding ASD methods by people working at commercial environments, concretely in the Brazilian market. A qualitative questionnaire was prepared and applied to 24 Information Technology professionals distributed across 5 states of Brazil. Results of the work show that although the participants are familiar with agile principles, they adopt few agile practices.

3   Methodology

A questionnaire containing 9 questions was devised in order to obtain information about the knowledge and the application of agile software development methods in research projects, which we consider as any project conducted with research purposes involving software development. The size of the software that is developed by the researchers was not considered relevant for this study, since the participants develop from small applications to big systems depending on the needs of their projects. The number of questions was selected aiming to keep simple the structure of the survey so that it could remain brief and user-friendly for the participants. Details about the building process of the survey and its application are discussed in this Section.

3.1   Building the Questionnaire

The questions of the survey were built by taking into account different aspects: knowledge about agile methods, application of agile methods, agreement with the agile principles and technical information about the researcher. The topics of each question of the questionnaire are explained next.

- Question 1: refers to whether the participant has insight into agile methods.
- Question 2: concerns the knowledge of the researcher about specific agile methods.
- Question 3: is related to which agile methods the researcher has ever applied for developing software in research projects.
- Question 4: inquires about which agile practices the researcher has ever applied in their research projects. This question is presented without mentioning the formal names of the practices since the researcher may have applied them (even partially) without knowing that they are part of some agile method.
- Question 5: refers to the agreement of the subject with each of the Agile Principles defined by the Agile Alliance [8]. Some of the Agile Principles are related to the relationship between the developers and the clients. Thus, we did not consider them for the questionnaire since they are not applicable to research projects.
- Question 6: this question has the same objective as Question 5 but instead of the Agile Principles from the Agile Alliance the question focuses on the Lean Software Development (LSD) principles Poppendieck [9].
- Question 7: inquires about to the openness of the subject to update his knowledge regarding software development.
- Questions 8 and 9: gather personal information as affiliation and line of research.

3.2 Applying the Questionnaire

The survey was made available on-line in Portuguese. The link of the questionnaire was sent through social media and e-mail. It was applied to 20 anonymous subjects chosen randomly from 9 laboratories from 7 Brazilian cities and one Australian city. The participants were MSc and Phd students, research professors working at universities, undergraduate students working on their final graduation projects and undergraduate students working as interns at laboratories. The education and experience of the participants, was very diverse, which was intentionally pursued in order to gather data from a very heterogeneous population. The individuals are not related to the agile community.

4   Results

This Section presents an analysis of the results obtained after the application of the questionnaire briefly described in Sect. 3.

A summary of the answers from the first question of the survey is shown in Fig. 1. The question refers to the basic knowledge of the participants about agile methods. Results show that 60% of the participants have deep knowledge about

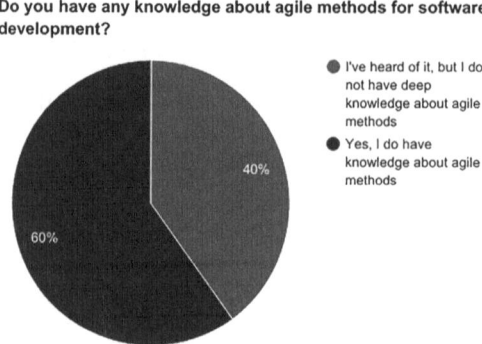

Fig. 1. Percentages of researchers that have knowledge about agile software development methods.

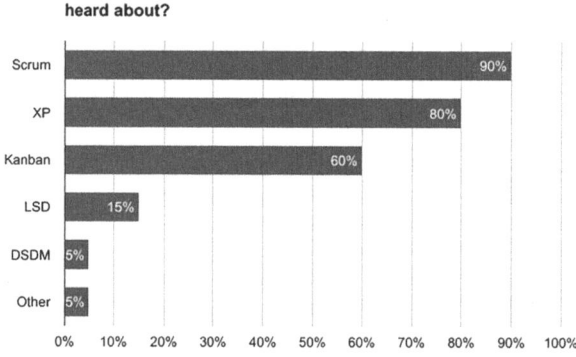

Fig. 2. Number of participants with knowledge about each agile method.

agile methods whilst the other 40% at least heard about them, although their knowledge is not too broad. There were no researchers stating that they have never heard about them, a sign of their spreading in the late years.

Results from the second question of the questionnaire, presented in Fig. 2, show that the most known method is Scrum, followed by XP. The first is known by 90% of the participants, whilst XP is known by 80%. This is similar to the results presented in a recent survey related to the state of the agile development [10], which states that Scrum is currently the most used method. The study also refers to a hybrid between XP and other methods as the second most used approach, which also correspond to the result obtained in this work. Kanban is in the third place of the list, since 60% of the participants know details or at least heard about the method. There is a significant difference between the first three methods, which we consider as the most known, and the remaining: LSD (15%), DSDM (5%) and Crystal (0%). One participant selected the option *Other*, adding the Planning Poker [11] practice as one of the methods he has

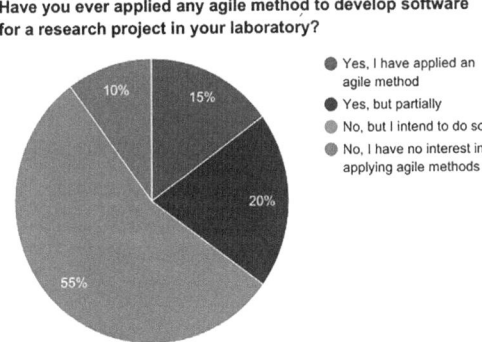

Fig. 3. Percentages of researchers that applied agile methods on their research projects.

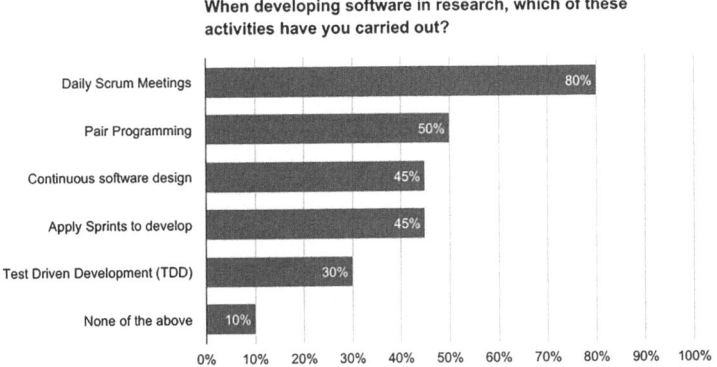

Fig. 4. Number of researchers that applied each agile practice in their research projects.

knowledge about, although it is a practice that commonly used within the scope of XP.

Results from the Question 3 are presented at Fig. 3. More than half of the participants (55%) stated that they have never applied agile methods to develop software for their research. Notwithstanding, they intend to apply them in future projects, even though they may not have much knowledge about them.

For Question 4, although we present the answers in the Fig. 4 with the formal names of the practices (e.g., Pair Programming or TDD), they were displayed in the questionnaire by using descriptions of them. Results for this question show that daily meetings to discuss issues about the software in development is a common task for the researchers. They may not be formal Daily Scrum Meetings, but the core activity (daily meetings to discuss aspects of the project) remains. Pair programming was the second most applied practice. It should also be treated as the practice discussed before: we consider that at least the core concept of the practice is applied. Incremental development (with Sprints or Iterations) and

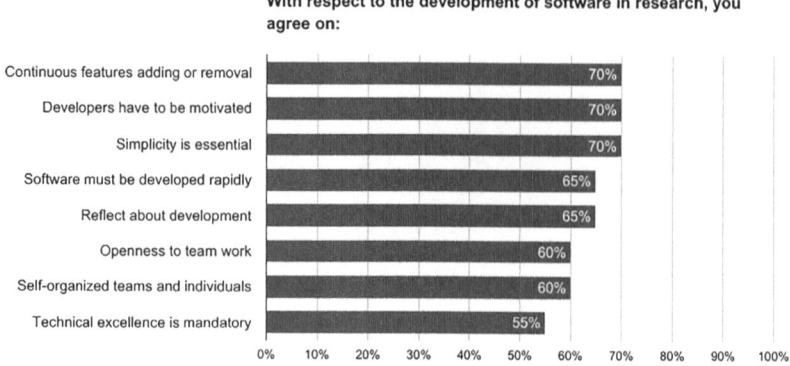

Fig. 5. Number of participants that agree with each agile principle of the Agile Alliance.

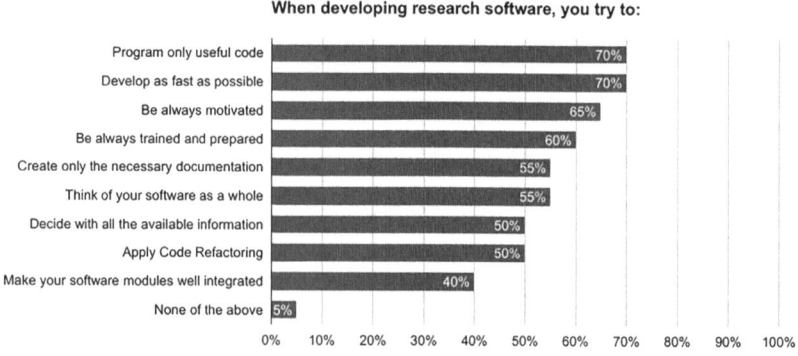

Fig. 6. Number of participants that agree with each of the LSD principles.

Continuous Software Design were the following practices, although with almost the same percentage as Pair Programming. Test Driven Development was the less applied practice. The use of Class Responsibility Collaborator (CRC) Cards [12] for software design was also an option for this question. However, none of the participants applied it.

Figure 5 presents results for the Question 5, which regards to the Agile Principles defined by the Agile Alliance [8]. At least more than 50% of the participants agree with each principle. The principle with less researchers support was the one stating that technical excellence is mandatory (55%) whilst the most supported principles are those related to the simplicity, continuous integration and motivation for develop, all three are supported by 70% of the participants. This shows that researchers tend to be pragmatic and that their projects requirements are usually dynamic.

Results related to the agreement with the LSD principles are presented in Fig. 6. As the Agile Alliance principles, there is consensus of the participants regarding the LSD principles (8 of the 9 principles have the support of at least 50% of the participants). However, the correct integration of the software modules does not seem to be so relevant for the researchers, since only 40% of the participants agree with it. Another important issue to point out is that 5% of the participants did not agree with any of the LSD principles.

As for the interest for updating their knowledge about software development, which results are shown in Fig. 7, most of the participants (55%) confirmed that they try to update their knowledge only when it is necessary for a project. A high percentage (40%) of participants also stated that they always try to keep updated whilst only 5% considers that it is not necessary. This shows that most researchers recognize that this is a crucial task for doing research.

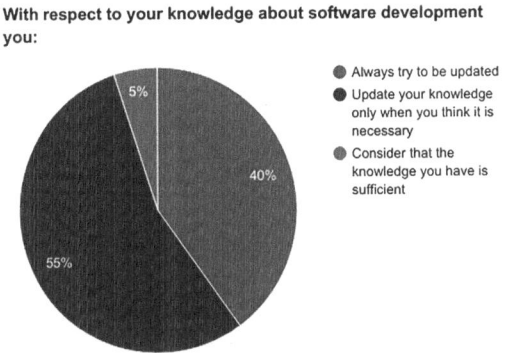

Fig. 7. Openness to update the knowledge regarding software development.

Fig. 8. Lines of research of the participants. The inferior axis presents the number of researchers working at each field.

Although all researchers develop software to a greater or lesser extent for their research projects or experiments, they work in different areas. Figure 8 presents their lines of research. In the survey, this question allowed the researcher to specify his line of research, which is why the figure presents a high number of research areas. The most common line of research is Computational Intelligence: 25% of the researchers work in that field.

4.1 Threats to Validity

The number of participants is a threat to validity of this work. We also consider that the backgrounds and research areas of the participants may bias the results of this work, since most were computer scientists. Future works may aim at collecting data from a bigger and more heterogeneous group of participants, they can also include non-Brazilian researchers, in order to obtain more general results.

5   Conclusion

This work aimed at studying the perception of researchers about the application of agile software development methods for research projects. Since, as far as we are aware of, there are no research has been published regarding the application of agile principles and practices in the research field, this study addressed this issue by constructing and applying a questionnaire to 20 researchers of diverse backgrounds that need to develop software for their projects.

Results show that researchers are open to apply Agile Software Development methods for their projects and that they already apply at least the core concepts of some agile practices. They also agree with the agile principles and exhibit openness to updating their knowledge regarding software development. The leading agile method is Scrum, followed by eXtreme Programming. The perception of researchers on applying agile software development methods on their projects is positive. There is a consensus regarding the benefits of agile development, since the participants demonstrated openness to apply agile practices and principles.

Taking these results into account, we can conclude that, in general, researchers consider Agile Methods as a viable option to develop software for their projects, since the software they develop usually have dynamic requirements and most of them already apply agile practices even without having formal knowledge about them. This positive response of the researchers may allow to carry more studies aiming at evaluating the application of ASD methods in research projects and their impact on the development process when compared to traditional methods.

For future works, the number of participants can be augmented along with the questions contained in the questionnaire. Another survey structure can also be applied by building one questionnaire for each agile method in order to obtain more specific results for each. The heterogeneity of the participants is another objective that can be pursued in future works, since the results presented in this document correspond to those obtained Brazilian researchers only. Thus, the survey can be also applied to participants from another countries.

References

1. Aitken, A., Ilango, V.: A comparative analysis of traditional software engineering and agile software development. In: Proceedings of the 2013 46th Hawaii International Conference on System Sciences, HICSS 2013, pp. 4751–4760. IEEE Computer Society, Washington, DC, USA (2013). ISBN: 978-0-7695-4892-0, https://doi.org/10.1109/HICSS.2013.31
2. Boehm, B., Turner, R.: Management challenges to implementing agile processes in traditional development organizations. IEEE Softw. **22**(5), 30–39 (2005). https://doi.org/10.1109/MS.2005.129. ISSN: 0740–7459
3. Conforto, E.C., Salum, F., Amaral, D.C., da Silva, S.L., de Almeida, L.F.M., Project Management Institute: Can agile project management be adopted by industries other than software development? Project Manage. J. **45**(3), 21–34 (2014). From Academia: Summaries of new research for the reflective practitioner
4. Turk, D., France, R., Rumpe, B.: Assumptions underlying agile software development processes (2014). arXiv preprint arXiv:1409.6610
5. Laanti, M., Salo, O., Abrahamsson, P.: Agile methods rapidly replacing traditional methods at Nokia: A survey of opinions on agile transformation. Inf. Softw. Technol. **53**(3), 276–290 (2011)
6. Rodríguez, P., Markkula, J., Oivo, M., Turula, K.: Survey on agile and lean usage in finnish software industry. In: Proceedings of the ACM-IEEE International Symposium on Empirical Software Engineering and Measurement, ESEM 2012, pp. 139–148. ACM, New York (2012). ISBN 978-1-4503-1056-7, https://doi.org/10.1145/2372251.2372275
7. Diel, E., Bergmann, M., Marczak, S., Luciano, E.: On the understanding of agile methods and their practice in Brazil. In: Workshop Brasileiro de Métodos Ageis, Florianópolis, Brazil (2014)
8. Beck, K., Beedle, M., van Bennekum, A., Cockburn, A., Cunningham, W., Fowler, M., Grenning, J., Highsmith, J., Hunt, A., Jeffries, R., Kern, J., Marick, B., Martin, R.C., Mallor, S., Shwaber, K., Sutherland, J.: The agile manifesto. Technical report, The Agile Alliance (2001)
9. Poppendieck, M.: Lean software development. In: Companion to the Proceedings of the 29th International Conference on Software Engineering, ICSE COMPANION 2007, pp. 165–166. IEEE Computer Society, Washington, DC, USA (2007). ISBN 0-7695-2892-9, https://doi.org/10.1109/ICSECOMPANION.2007.46
10. VersionOne: State of Agile Development (2010). http://stateofagile.versionone.com/
11. Cohn, M.: Agile Estimating and Planning. Prentice Hall PTR, Upper Saddle River (2005)
12. Beck, K., Cunningham, W.: A laboratory for teaching object oriented thinking. SIGPLAN Not. 24(10), 1–6 (1989). ISSN 0362–1340, https://doi.org/10.1145/74878.74879

Mob Programming: The State of the Art and Three Case Studies of Open Source Software

Herez Moise Kattan[1]([✉]), Frederico Oliveira[2], Alfredo Goldman[1],
and Joseph William Yoder[3]

[1] Department of Computer Science, Institute of Mathematics and Statistics
of the University of Sao Paulo (IME-USP), Sao Paulo, Sao Paulo, Brazil
{herez,gold}@ime.usp.br
[2] Samsung SIDI Institute, Campinas, Sao Paulo, Brazil
f.oliveira@samsung.com
[3] The Refactory, Inc., Urbana, IL, USA
joe@joeyoder.com

Abstract. Mob programming is a whole team technique that includes programmers and others such as product owners or testers working together in the same space and time, discussing solutions and writing code in a fast succession on a shared screen and keyboard. This paper includes a literature review and case studies of Mob Programming in software development of three open source software in an academic setting. Aspects and practices involved in the Mob Programming are analyzed. The identification of common practices can serve as standards in the Mob Programming sessions. We carried out experiments with teams practicing this technique. The bond formed among the members were the strengths of the three teams experience. The noise from work in an open room irritated two members, but two members of the same team did not get bothered and was not a problem for the remaining ten other participants. The approval of Mob Programming was unanimous in each retrospective. Providing the infrastructure to use more computers could be useful for parallel searches when a task on the Mob Programming computer takes too long, or when the team needs learn new technologies. We conclude that improved the team learning.

Keywords: Collaboration in software development · Agile practice
Programming teams · Programming technique
Software development approach · Mob programming

1   Introduction

Mob Programming is a software development approach where the whole team works on the same thing, at the same time, in the same space, and at the same computer [1]. Mob Programming, as Zuill [1] describes, is similar to pair programming [3], where two persons work on the same computer and collaborate on the same code at the same time.

© Springer International Publishing AG 2018
V. A. Santos et al. (Eds.): WBMA 2017, CCIS 802, pp. 146–160, 2018.
https://doi.org/10.1007/978-3-319-73673-0_12

The main difference, compared to pair programming is that the whole team works together as part of the pairing. In addition to software coding, Mob Programming teams work together on almost all tasks that a typical software development team tackles, such as defining stories, designing, testing, deploying software, and collaborating with the customer [1].

Since the popularization of Mob Programming by Zuill [1] there has been Mob sessions experiences described in some papers [1,5,11–13,15,17,18]. Mob Programming techniques also resembles the Randori [4] style of programming popular at Coding Dojos commonly used during sessions to learn new technologies and techniques [5].

This report describes common practices that could serve as standards in the Mob Programming sessions. We reviewed the most relevant Mob Programming literature and carried out experiments with teams practicing the technique. Our motivation is to find a way to develop quality software in the most productive way possible. The goal of this paper is to deepen the knowledge about Mob Programming by the conduction of case studies in an academic setting with three different teams and discover what we could learn about Mob Programming in practice.

2 Research Method and Organization of the Work

The authors have experience practicing Mob Programming [16]. The scope of the research involved a review of the literature and application examples to learn in the practice [6–8]. The literature review aimed to identify, analyze, interpret and report the relevant studies available to answer the research question "What are the practices used in the industry on Mob Programming?".

The sources of the search for this paper are IEEE Xplore (ieeexplore.ieee.org), ACM Digital Library (dl.acm.org), SpringerLink (springerlink.com), Elsevier, others websites like Agile Alliance, Google, and Portal for Periodicals of the CAPES (periodicos.capes.gov.br). The search string used was 'Mob Programming' that found thirteen studies, that were evaluated based on the inclusion and exclusion criteria described in Table 1, with emphasis on EC3, to exclude abstracts and slides. The eight accepted papers passed in all inclusion criteria and the five rejected papers did fail in either one of the exclusion criteria.

We conducted Case Studies of Mob Programming with three teams in an academic setting, trying to validate the literature findings and also to provide

Table 1. Inclusion and exclusion criteria.

Inclusion criteria	Exclusion criteria
IC1. Studies about Mob Programming, including grey literature [9]	EC1. Repeated studies
IC2. Studies applied in industry	EC2. Incomplete studies and drafts
IC3. Qualitative or quantitative research	EC3. Slides and abstracts

new insights. We looked for common aspects and practices involved. The Participant Selection process was: who had enrollment at LabXP and voluntarily did accept to collaborate with this research. Fourteen people participated, thirteen men, and only one woman. The fourteen people were members of the three teams and answered all the questions, twelve individual questions, and forty-one team questions (two questionnaires). The response rate for the survey was 100%.

The survey design split into two parts, a first about one questionnaire with individual questions, and a second with questions thought to the team, looking for examining their experience practicing Mob Programming about relevant aspects described in the literature.

The first questionnaire got fifty-six individual answers of the all fourteen participants. The team questions of the second got one hundred twenty-three answers of the three teams. Below are more details about the two questionnaires.

Individual Questions of the First Questionnaire:

- How many years have you been programming? (educational and professional experience in any language)
- How do you evaluate your current level of knowledge in the programming language used currently?
- Do you like Mob Programming? Did you Have practical experience with Mob Programming before this course?
- How would you compare Mob Programming with other practices?

The Second Questionnaire is About the Experience with Mob Programming at LAB XP Was Answered by Each Team and Had Questions Related to:

- The setup of the room and also a description of the Mob setting;
- Driver rotation;
- Retrospectives and mini-retrospectives;
- Automation of the job;
- Avoiding idle time;
- Learning as a team;
- Groupthink;
- Collective intelligence;
- Learning and mentoring;
- Continuous Improvement.

All projects are open source. The consent term, photos, two questionnaires and all answers of the fourteen members of the three teams are available online at the IME-USP CCSL Wiki [28].

The paper has six sections. The literature review is following, in the next section, and looking for aspects related to Mob Programming. In the fourth section, are the details of the case studies. After that, in the fifth section, is the analysis of the results. In the last section of this paper, we conclude and address the limitations. The acknowledgments are in the end before the references.

3   State of the Art

We review the literature of Mob Programming looking for patterns of relevant aspects and practices involved most frequently used that guided the case studies. The next subsection is the background. Subsequently, Mob Programming aspects are analyzed.

3.1   Background

Tens and hundreds of interactions between people occur every day in their work. The people express ideas, discuss problems, explore possible solutions, and share thoughts all day long. To make it possible and to keep this high level of communication happening throughout the day, the team must adopt the principle of treating each other with kindness, consideration, and respect [1].

Retrospectives are used in Mob Programming sessions [1]. In these ceremonies, the team frequently evaluates what is working for them, what problems they might be having, and how they can improve. These are usually quick and focused on one item.

A possibility to Mob Programming is adopting the Driver/Navigators pattern adapted from Llewellyn Falco's "strong" pair programming style [10]. The basic rule is for an idea to go from your head into the computer it MUST go through someone else's hands.

There are two roles: the Driver, and the Navigator. The Driver has the possession of the keyboard. The Navigators discuss the idea being coded and guide the Driver in creating the code [1].

The team adopting Mob Programming has the possibility of a timed rotation. Each team member plays the role of Driver with the possession of the keyboard for a short time. The timer remembers the current driver when can pass the possession of the keyboard to the next driver when their turn ends up [1].

Another important aspect is the configuration of the room. The room must be physically comfortable while the team members work relatively close to each other, using shared monitors, keyboards, computer setup, and programming tools. There is only one computer in use for programming [1].

A set up of the room possible is two projectors or monitors. The goal is to keep the screens at about the same size, general position, resolution, and brightness to make them comfortable to work with all day long. There are also two keyboards and two mouses (a simple one and another ergonomic one).

Everyone has the choice to suit him/herself in the better way. Each team member has its own chair which is moved around on the different roles (Driver or Navigator). Thus, the people not need constantly readjust the chair settings making each one stay as comfortable as possible [2].

Finally, the room has a rolling magnetic whiteboard to keep track the work in an informative workspace. Figure 1 illustrates a setup that worked very well and had been seen it at some companies [2]. A possibility is to have one, two, or more monitors. The readjustment of the monitor height to be a height suitable for everyone.

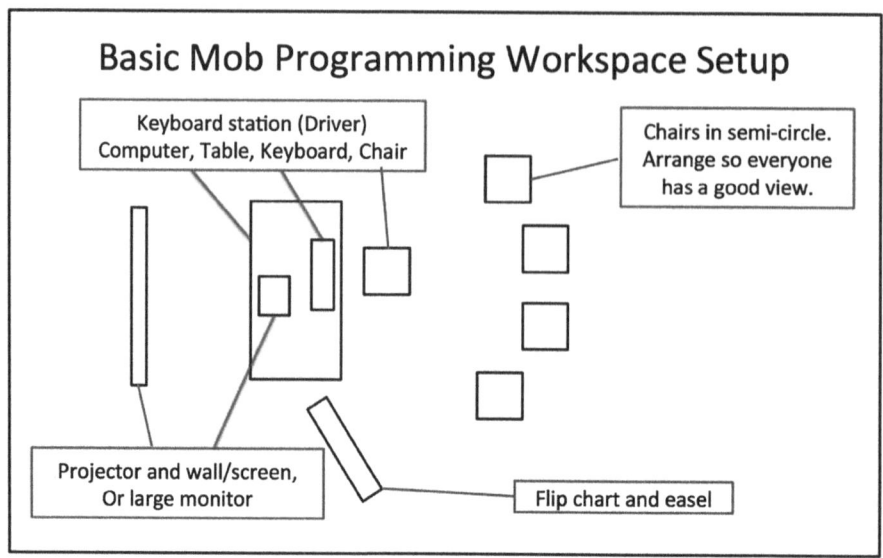

Fig. 1. A setup that has been used it at some companies [2].

3.2   Aspects and Practices Involved in Mob Programming

Here, we present the results of the literature review about aspects and practices involved in Mob Programming. Table 2 is a correlation of the selected papers for this study and all others papers. We only consider a common aspect when is cited in at least two papers.

Table 2. Practices versus papers.

Aspect or practice	[1]	[5]	[11]	[12]	[13]	[15]	[17]	[18]
Room setup	X	X	X	X	X	X		
Driver rotation	X	X	X	X	X		X	X
Retrospectives	X	X	X	X				
Automation		X	X					
Structured breaks				X	X			

Setup of the Room. The setup of the room is one of the pillars of Mob Programming [1] and the configurations are described in details by all papers [1,5,11–13,15].

According to Boekhout [12], the team found the screen too small, so it was hard to get everyone in a position near enough to it, due to all the desks. Distractions from outside were an issue that causes many interruptions. They have

Fig. 2. The setup of the room using one projector [12].

a room designed for training that was a little more isolated, with fewer interruptions, a projector and a big monitor for presentations. The team quickly discovered that the resolution of the projector was low and harmful. A high-resolution projector is a suitable solution. Then they had to use the big monitor. The team also decided to use proper office chairs, and have everybody move around keeping their chair to save time and avoid continuously fiddling with the chair configuration. Figure 2 illustrates a setup of the room using one projector.

Wilson [5] also describes an issue about the lower resolution of television or projector. The solution was to supplement paired workstation with an additional 50-in monitor that was a mirror of the workstation screen. It has been placed at right angles to the actual monitor, with the intention of the team watching the big screen and the driver can see both the screen and the rest of the team. Figure 3 illustrates this possible configuration.

Driver Rotation. In the opinion of Wilson [5], the ideal time of rotation for a Mob of 4–6 people seems to be 5 min. But, for a Mob of 3 people, ten minutes was more appropriate.

In the report of Kerney [11], a team consisting of five people rotates who has the possession of the keyboard at each fifteen minutes. But, not always means that the team must rotate when the timer is up, the team decides in each case and sometimes not use fifteen-minute rotations. Change the time of rotation in special circumstances, such as for visitors or learning sessions.

Fig. 3. Running a four people mob. The driver is in the background [5].

In the report of Boekhout [12], the team copying Woody's video [19] started with a rotation of ten minutes. Unfortunately, it seemed to them that every change of driver and navigator became an interruption and it took the team time to get back to focus on the problem at hand. There was clearly no sign of flow. So, they followed a tip that Boekhout [12] got from Llewellyn at Agile 2015 [33] and proved to be very important: lower the rotation cycle from ten to four minutes. By rotating so quickly, the switch has to go smoothly, so that you really need to make sure the workspace is good, you have a good timer and most important, that everybody is fully involved all the time. After a while, another team slowed to five minutes and declared that worked better for them too.

Retrospectives. In the view of Zuill [1], the team always looks for 'action items', and limit themselves to only one or two that they can use to 'tune and adjust' the process. They have found that having more than one or two 'action items' is almost always counter-productive. The team also set aside from half an hour to an hour to reflect on the last week or two. In these sessions, they gather information on sticky notes, do affinity groupings, dot-voting, and have conversations about the things they have observed and new things they would like to try.

There are also Just-In-Time Ad-hoc retrospectives. When anyone on the team notices something they feel we should reflect on, the team simply go ahead and

Fig. 4. An early task and retro board - notice the focus on the hourly retro [12].

do it while the experience is fresh. These are usually quick and focused on one item [14].

Kerney [11] described that the team does the retrospectives immediately when they found a problem. For example, the team realized that the projectors they had were constantly going dim, and it made the text hard to read. The immediately team tried several adjustments to fix it until they found a solution.

According to Boekhout [12], a core practice for the teams was the hourly retrospectives. An hourly retro needs to be short and to go to-the-point. The team started with a simple positive/negative items system and made sure this was visualized on their daily scrum board. Figure 4 illustrates this board.

The Fig. 4 shows the basis of the board is the horizontal axis for the hourly blocks. According to Boekhout, every hour the corresponding column is used. The top part for positive, the lower part of the improvements. The left of the board is a basic scrum board (To Do/In Progress/Done), turned on its side, where the team keeps track of the tasks about the user story of the day [12].

Automation. Kerney [11] mentioned that the team strives to make things as fluid as possible so that they do not have to break their flow. Some benefits as such as the team have an environment that is easy to maintain, and people cannot focus all the time on something that is tedious.

Structured Breaks. According to Boekhout [12] and Griffith [13], full involvement all the time can be exhausting. So the team made sure that every hour there was a 5–10 min break after the retrospective where people weren't allowed to be behind the screen. Even then a full day can feel like a marathon [12].

4   Case Studies of Open Source Software

The programmers are attendees of LABXP, a regular course offered by the University of Sao Paulo, to graduate and undergraduate Computer Science students. First, the teams watched a lecture about Mob Programming with Alfredo Goldman and Joseph Yoder. They showed one video to the attendees about the time-lapse of a full day of work of a team of Mob Programmers [19].

The course requires a minimum of at least eight hours per week of dedication, and there is a lunch once a week, to allow the students to share experiences. The conduction of these examples of Mob Programming application in an academic setting with three different teams began in 08/08/2016 and finished on 12/12/2016. All the projects are open source. A questionnaire was applied to deepen the knowledge about the experience of the fourteen team members.

4.1   GeoXPerience: gitlab.com/geoxperience

A georeferencing platform for Casa dos Meninos, a social project [27]. It is a web georeferencing system that allows the user to create customized maps [26].

The website through a CSV file upload latitude and longitude data on a map to show the coordinates of the Basic Health Units of the City of Sao Paulo, as well as any other point on the map of interest of the user.

4.2   The Game of Life: github.com/Automata-Life

Automata.Life is a multiplayer web-based game based on JohnConway's Game of Life where several players need to fight for the survival of their single-celled species in an arena like Agar.io.

You can 'program' your cells to better try to dominate your space, or yield under the forces of Darwinism [24,25].

Figure 5 is a photo of the team of the game of life working in the programming, note that they are using a laser pointer, making easier to point an issue in the source code to be fixed. They had two projectors available and computers to parallel searches.

4.3   Mezuro: mezuro.org

Mezuro is a free/libre web platform for collaborative source code evaluation. Able to evaluate source code with the most popular SCMs (like Git and SVN), just by providing its URL.

For now, it can evaluate C, C++, Java, Ruby, Python, and PHP source codes, but the Mezuro team are looking forward to supporting more languages in the future. Mezuro is continuously under development [20–23].

Fig. 5. The team of the game of life is working in the programming, note that they are using a laser pointer, making easier to point an issue in the source code to be fixed.

4.4   Questionnaire: ccsl.ime.usp.br/wiki/SwarmQuestionnaire

Consent term, photos, two questionnaires and all answers of the fourteen members of the three teams, are available online at the CCSL Wiki of the IME-USP [28].

5   Result Analysis

Table 3 correlates the answers of the questionnaires with the aspects that were considered relevant by previous works and explanations emerged using the axial code technique of Grounded Theory.

During all process, we (the researchers) takes photos and wrote memos. These memos contain the key points observed to help us in their categorization. After, we reviewed again the literature looking for answers that would contribute to formulating a theory based on the results produced by the questionnaires and metrics. Figure 6 shows the programming experience of all the fourteen members (thirteen men and one woman).

Mob Programming reflects very well the Weinberg [32] idea of ego-less programming, where the software is owned by the team as a whole, instead of the individuals being responsible for problems with the code.

Table 3. The answers that justify the aspects and new insights.

Aspects	The answers that justify the aspect
Room setup	Sometimes, a team member was able to help a member from another group due to the shared room. The noise from work in an open room irritated two members, but two members of the same team did not get bothered and was not a problem for the remaining ten other participants. The team of Automata.Life worked with two projectors and more computers available to use if needed. The team of GeoXperience worked with one projector and two notebooks available to use. The team of Mezuro worked with one big screen television and more computers and notebooks available to use
Kindness and respect	The bond formed among the members were the strengths of the three teams experience
The Driver/Navigators Pattern	Automata.Live team used the laser pointer during some work sessions to the navigators communicate with the driver. GeoXPerience team said that the laser pointer is a good idea. Mezuro team members usually stand up to show something with the hand on television to the entire team
Automation	The team of Automata.Live automated the timer, build, test, and deploy processes. They did it because those tools helped them perform daily tasks. The Mezuro team tried to reduce wasted time by making use of our text editor's automated functionalities (Vim of Linux). Furthermore, they frequently used shell commands to speed up some processes. The GeoXPerience team automated the tests and CI and reported that was useful, and would have been more productive if they had automated more stuff
Retrospectives	They did daily mini-retrospectives, a mid-project retrospective with Professor Alfredo, and technical retrospectives with Joe Yoder, coaching all the three teams
Structured Breaks	They like to have spontaneous breaks, where the team members usually left to and came back from the breaks individually. Thus, was valued individual freedom of choice of breaks and the team continues to make progress even when individuals left for having a break. So, occurred few structured team breaks
Driver rotation	All teams developed their own timer tool, which received an integer as argument and warned them when the time was up. They enjoyed because it helped us organized the rotation, typically used 15–20 min. Automata.Live and Mezuro teams were able to use the Strong Style at some points. Automata.Live had difficulty enforcing it all the time because found it difficult to force the rotation when the current driver had an idea to solve the problem, but they were able to do that sometimes. Mezuro team used more the Strong Style with a timer to Driver rotation
Others Computers	Providing the infrastructure to use more computers could be useful for parallel searches when a task on the Mob Programming computer takes too long, or when the team needs learn new technologies
Using Mob Programming is not advantageous in doubt moments	When no one of the team knows a specific technology, it is better to do individuals searches to learn and after regroup again. Mezuro: *"There are some tasks that the team does not seem fit for Mob Programming all the times. The solving of some DevOps tasks were improved using Mob Programming, but others not so much. Especially the ones which the team did not know what to do for sure and the approach was trial and error"*
Sharing knowledge	The capacity to distribute the knowledge through a streamlined method and working with friends, we observed that increased the learning
Developers approved and enjoyed	The fourteen members of the three teams approved and enjoyed. Mezuro: *"Yes. The approval of Mob Programming was unanimous at every retrospective"*

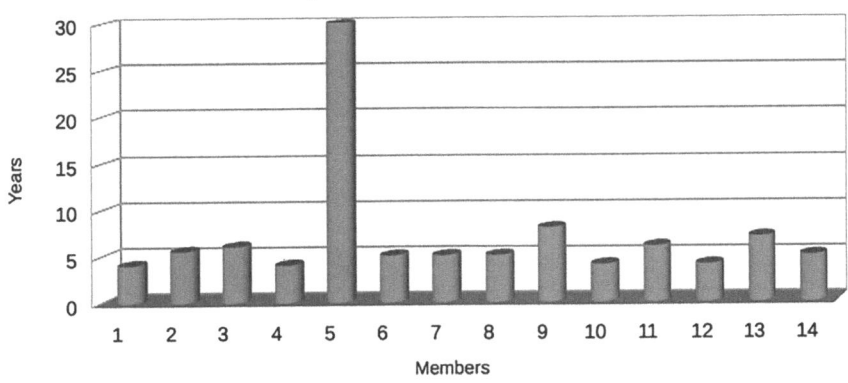

Fig. 6. Programming experience of team members.

Fig. 7. One member of the team is pointing with the hands an issue in the source code.

We agree that different types of collaboration are suited to different kinds of problems. If the particular problem stem from the team not having a shared understanding of the project, Mob Programming that involve the entire team is a great approach [1,5,11–13,15,16,29]. Western Electric made experiments attempted to determine the relationship between light levels and worker efficiency. The data compiled by the Illumination Experiments indicated only a minor correlation between light levels and worker productivity [30]. However, one interesting observation is sometimes when increasing the light level, the productivity grows up and when decrease the light level the productivity grow up too. Thus, the light experiment showed that **increased interest of the workers** increased productivity. Mob Programming increase the satisfaction, bond among team members, and learning of the software developer. These are factors of productivity that could justify the use of Mob Programming.

Mob Programming in an open work-space environment increases the Integration Among Teams in the LABXP course, that is one relevant factor to Inter-team Knowledge Sharing and open work-space environment provide great value, but software developers have to deal with the problem of noise [31].

Overall, there was a very positive experience to all teams. Figure 7 is showing the team of the Mezuro working in the programming. In the photo, one member of the team is pointing with the hands, an issue in the source code. A laser-pointer seems to be a good idea.

6   Conclusion and Limitations

We confirm the literature reviewed about the advantages of the use of Mob Programming over other techniques to sharing knowledge, learning, and satisfaction of the programmer. We also confirm that sometimes it is better to alternate with other techniques like pair programming. Additionally, we noted that collaboration among teams is improved and the bond formed among the team members.

Our answers to questionnaire did not confirm the literature that most programmers have practically non-existent moments of frustration in a Mob Programming session. We observed that in moments when nobody of the team knows a tool/framework was exhaustive to the whole group to approach these situations. When no one of the team knows a specific technology, it is better to do individuals searches to learn and after regroup again.

Limitations. The case studies performed are a qualitative research strategy and not permit generalizations, but all our data (source code hosted at Gitlab or Github, metrics, and questionnaires) are open source, thus could be audited. Our questionnaire is very extensive because we tried to confirm all details observed, these data are auditable observations available publicly in the Wiki.

Acknowledgments. Authors would like to thank the CAPES and the IME-USP.

References

1. Zuill, W.: Mob Programming: A Whole Team Approach. Experience report, Agile (2014). https://www.agilealliance.org/resources/experience-reports/mob-programming-whole-team-approach-woody-zuill/
2. Zuill, W., Meadows, K.: Mob Programming - A Whole Team Approach. This book is 95% complete (2016). http://leanpub.com/mobprogramming. Last Updated on 29 Oct 2016
3. Beck, K., Andres, C.: Extreme Programming Explained: Embrace Change, 2nd edn. Addison-Wesley, Boston (2004). 75 p
4. Rooksby, J., Hunt, J., Wang, X.: The theory and practice of randori coding dojos. In: Cantone, G., Marchesi, M. (eds.) XP 2014. LNBIP, vol. 179, pp. 251–259. Springer, Cham (2014). https://doi.org/10.1007/978-3-319-06862-6_18
5. Wilson, A.: Mob programming - what works, what doesn't. In: Lassenius, C., Dingsøyr, T., Paasivaara, M. (eds.) XP 2015. LNBIP, vol. 212, pp. 319–325. Springer, Cham (2015). https://doi.org/10.1007/978-3-319-18612-2_33
6. Kattan, H.M.: Illuminated arrow: a research method to software engineering based on action research, systematic review and grounded theory. In: CONTECSI 2016, 13th International Conference on Information Systems and Technology Management, Paper submission: 1 Dec 2015 - Presented at Session4A - AUD Systems Auditing and IT Governance 02 Jun 2016-15H30, pp. 1971–1978 (2016). https://doi.org/10.5748/9788599693124-13CONTECSI/PS-3926
7. Kattan, H.M.: Those who fail to learn from history are doomed to repeat it. In: Agile Processes in Software Engineering and Extreme Programming: Poster Presented at the 18th International Conference on Agile Software Development, XP 2017, Held in Cologne, Germany, 22–26 May 2017 (2017). https://doi.org/10.13140/RG.2.2.20864.02563
8. Moise Kattan, H., Goldman, A.: Software development practices patterns. In: Baumeister, H., Lichter, H., Riebisch, M. (eds.) XP 2017. LNBIP, vol. 283, pp. 298–303. Springer, Cham (2017). https://doi.org/10.1007/978-3-319-57633-6_23
9. Schöpfel, J.: Towards a prague definition of grey literature. In: Proceedings of the Twelfth International Conference on Grey Literature: Transparency in Grey Literature. Grey Tech Approaches to High Tech Issues, Prague, December 6–7 (2010)
10. Falco, L.: Llewellyn's strong-style pairing (2014). http://llewellynfalco.blogspot.com.br/2014/06/llewellyns-strong-style-pairing.html
11. Kerney, J.: Mob Programming - My first team. Experience report, via Initiative of Agile Alliance (2016)
12. Boekhout, K.: Mob programming: find fun faster. In: Sharp, H., Hall, T. (eds.) XP 2016. LNBIP, vol. 251, pp. 185–192. Springer, Cham (2016). https://doi.org/10.1007/978-3-319-33515-5_15
13. Griffith, A.: Mob Programming for the Introverted. Experience report, Agile (2016)
14. Arsenovski, D.: Swarm: beyond pair, beyond Scrum. Experience report, Agile (2016)
15. Hohman, M., Slocum, A.: Mob Programming and the Transition to XP (2001)
16. Kattan, H.M.: Programming and review simultaneous in pairs: a pair programming extension. Master dissertation, Institute for Technological Research of the Sao Paulo State (2015). http://aleph.ipt.br/F or http://ipt.br, click on: Online Consultations, then click on: Library. https://doi.org/10.13140/RG.2.2.15831.68004

17. Lilienthal, C.: From pair programming to mob programming to mob architecting. In: Winkler, D., Biffl, S., Bergsmann, J. (eds.) SWQD 2017. LNBIP, vol. 269, pp. 3–12. Springer, Cham (2017). https://doi.org/10.1007/978-3-319-49421-0_1
18. Balijepally V., Chaudhry S., Nerur S.: Mob programming - a promising innovation in the agile toolkit. In: Twenty-third Americas Conference on Information Systems, Boston (2017)
19. Zuill, W.: A Day of Mob Programming (2012). https://www.youtube.com/watch?v=p_pvslS4gEI
20. Mezuro Wiki. http://ccsl.ime.usp.br/wiki/Mezuro
21. Mezuro. http://Mezuro.org
22. Mezuro GitLab. http://gitlab.com/mezuro
23. Mezuro GitHub. http://github.com/mezuro
24. The Game of Life Wiki. http://ccsl.ime.usp.br/wiki/Automata.Life
25. The Game of Life GitHub. http://github.com/Automata-Life
26. GeoXP: http://ccsl.ime.usp.br/wiki/Sistema_online_de_georreferenciamento
27. GeoXP GitLab. http://gitlab.com/geoxperience
28. Questionnaire. http://ccsl.ime.usp.br/wiki/SwarmQuestionnaire
29. GDS post. http://gds.blog.gov.uk/2016/09/01/using-mob-programming-to-solve-a-problem/
30. Western Electric Company Hawthorne Studies Collection, Baker Library, Harvard Business School. http://oasis.lib.harvard.edu/oasis/deliver/~bak00047
31. Santos, V., Goldman, A., Souza, C.: Fostering effective inter-team knowledge sharing in agile software development. Empir. Softw. Eng. **20**, 1006–1051 (2015)
32. Weinberg, G.: The Psychology of Computer Programming. Van Nostrand, New York (1971)
33. Falco, L.: Group Learning. Today's exercise: Unit Testing. Session at Agile (2015)

Author Index